COPYRIGHT

Text and photographs copyright © 2016 by Jared Flood

All rights reserved. No part of this publication may be reproduced, distributed or transmitted in any form or by any means, including photocopying or other electronic methods without written permission from the author.

ORDERING INFORMATION

Interested in stocking this book in your bookstore or yarn shop? Wholesale inquiries may be submitted via email to the address below.

Published by Brooklyn Tweed
www.brooklyntweed.com
wholesale@brooklyntweed.com

PRINTED IN THE USA

This book is printed on Forest Stewardship Council® certified paper. FSC® certification ensures that the paper in this publication contains fibers from well managed and responsibly harvested forests that meet strict environmental and socioeconomic standards.

ISBN: 978-0-9976273-0-5

FIRST EDITION

Third Printing
December 2016

WOOLENS

A BOOK OF KNITTED ACCESSORIES

by Jared Flood

TABLE OF
Contents

LETTER
7

PATTERNS
33

JOURNAL
118

TECHNIQUES
122

ABBREVIATIONS
134

CROSSHATCH
scarf

10 | 34

TRAVELER
cowl

12 | 40

HALO
shawl

14 | 48

FAR HILLS
scarf

16 | 56

SEEDS
hat

18 | 64

TABLE OF

Contents

TESSERA	BYWAY	FAR HILLS
cowl	*scarf*	*hat*
20 | 72	22 | 78	24 | 86

REDSHIFT	FURROW	FURROW
shawl	*cowl*	*hat*
26 | 92	28 | 100	30 | 106

LETTER

When I first took up knitting, my earliest finished project was a wool beanie, knit circularly with a ribbed brim and a simple striping pattern in black and grey. I remember how much I loved experiencing the arc of the knitting process, from cast-on to bind-off, over the short span of a few days. Enjoying the spoils of my handwork brought a deep sense of satisfaction and spurred me on to more projects.

The simple pleasure of making accessories is still something that drives my knitting, almost 15 years later. And while I consider myself a devout sweater knitter, I've found that the smaller projects — those that spontaneously bring new yarns, textures and ideas into my hands — contribute in equal part to my enjoyment of our craft.

This book celebrates our impromptu knitting detours: a last-minute birthday hat for a dear friend, a toasty cowl to match your new winter coat, a shawl whose yardage requirements are perfect for that beloved new addition to your yarn stash, or an excuse for a short respite from the 80+ hours you've logged on that epic cabled sweater in your knitting basket. Most of the patterns in this book have been designed to give you choices — of color, finished dimensions, design features and yarn weight — and my hope is that you'll use them as jumping-off points to create engaging projects that make you happy you're a knitter.

All my very best,

JARED FLOOD

KNIT DESIGNS

CROSSHATCH
SCARF

—

p. 34

TRAVELER

COWL

—

p. 40

HALO
SHAWL

—

p. 48

FAR HILLS
SCARF

—

p. 56

SEEDS

HAT

—

p. 64

TESSERA

COWL

—

p. 72

BYWAY
SCARF

—

p. 78

FAR HILLS

HAT

—

p. 86

FURROW
COWL
—
p. 100

FURROW

HAT

—

p. 106

KNITTING PATTERNS

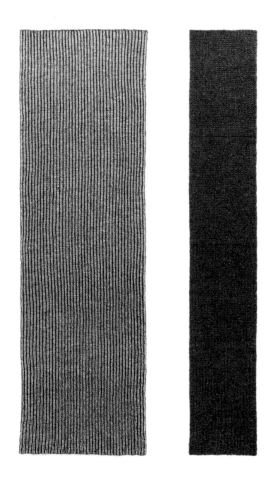

CROSSHATCH SCARF

Crosshatch is a great example of how an old standby like brioche stitch can look new again when you create the fabric with two different weights of yarn in contrasting colors. Each pair of rows alternates between a worsted and fingering weight to create a woven herringbone effect. During finishing the scarf is stretch-blocked with blocking wires — further opening the stitch pattern — to achieve a fabric with beautiful drape.

SPREAD	SCHEMATIC	PATTERN
10	36	37

CROSSHATCH

Overview

MATERIALS

Scarf Version (Wrap Version)
- Worsted: 385 (715) yards of worsted weight wool yarn in Color 1 (C1)
- Fingering: 495 (905) yards of fingering weight wool yarn in Color 2 (C2)

3 (6) skeins of Brooklyn Tweed *Shelter* (100% American Targhee-Columbia wool; 140 yards/50g)
2 (4) skeins of Brooklyn Tweed *Loft* (100% American Targhee-Columbia wool; 275 yards/50g)
Scarf photographed in colors Old World (C1) & Artifact (C2) and Wrap photographed in colors Cast Iron (C1) & Fossil (C2)

GAUGE

13 stitches & 40 rows = 4" in Brioche Stitch with Size A needle(s), after stretch-blocking
Note that for Brioche Stitch, each elongated stitch in a column of knit stitches represents two rows; when you count these it will appear that 20 rows = 4"

NEEDLES

Size A (for Brioche Fabric)
One 32" circular needle* in size needed to obtain gauge listed
Suggested Size: 4 mm (US 6)

Size B (for Tubular Cast On; optional)
One 32" circular needle* one size smaller than Size A
Suggested Size: 3¾ mm (US 5)

*A circular needle is required in order to slide the piece back and forth when working the stitch pattern.
If you have adjusted the needle size to obtain the correct gauge, it may or may not be necessary to make a matching adjustment to the needle size used for Tubular Cast On due to variance in individual work. You may wish to test your chosen cast-on method on your swatch.

DIMENSIONS

13¼ (25½)" [33.5 (65) cm] wide
76¼" [193.5 cm] long
Measurements taken from relaxed fabric after stretch-blocking

TOOLS

Blunt tapestry needle, locking markers, T-pins, blocking wires (optional)
If working Tubular Cast On, you will also require smooth waste yarn (sport- or DK-weight cotton, silk, or bamboo yarn) and Size B needle. You may use another cast on if desired, omitting these tools.

●●●○○
SKILL LEVEL

Intermediate
Knitter's choice of cast on, two-color brioche knitting, tubular cast on instructions provided

CROSSHATCH
Schematic

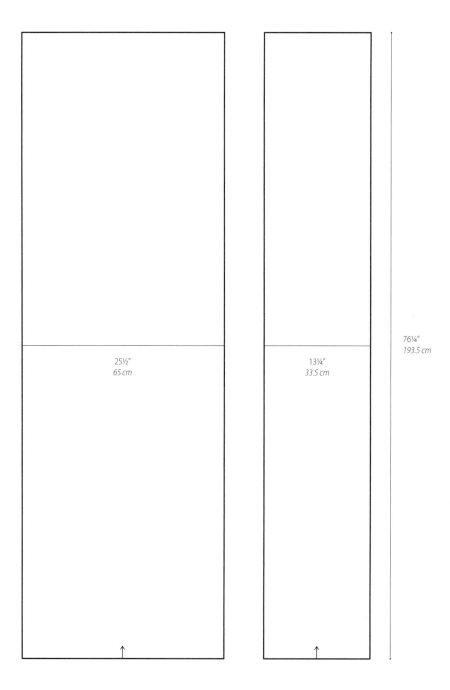

CROSSHATCH

Pattern

CONSTRUCTION NOTES

- Both scarf and wrap versions are worked from end to end with two weights of yarn used alternately—one strand of worsted weight and one strand of fingering weight.
- It is important that the tension of the cast-on and bind-off edges be compatible with the gauge of the fabric. Test the method and needle size used on your gauge swatch to ensure a successful outcome.
- Instructions for the scarf version appear first, followed by the wrap version in parentheses. If only one figure appears, it applies to both versions.
- For best results, wet-block piece using blocking wires to straighten edges and align corners (see Techniques section, p. 132).

STITCH PATTERN CHOICES

This pattern allows you to choose between two different selvedge treatments, provided below. You may wish to try both on your swatch before choosing which one you'd like to use for your scarf.

Brioche Stitch with Garter Selvedges
Odd number of stitches; 4-row repeat

This selvedge treatment is easy to work and to memorize.

Cast on with C1 (worsted weight), then slide the stitches back to other end of needle so that C1 is hanging at the L edge (you will begin with C2 (fingering weight) at the R edge).

Setup Row (RS): With C2 (fingering weight), knit 1, *purl 1, Yf-Sl1-YOF; repeat from * to last 2 stitches, purl 1, knit 1.

Row 1A (WS): With C1 (worsted weight), purl 1, *Yf-Sl1-YOF, BRP; repeat from * to last 2 stitches, Yf-Sl1-YOF, purl 1. Slide stitches back to other end of needle to work another WS row.
Row 1B (WS): With C2, knit 1, *BRK, Yf-Sl1-YO; repeat from * to last 2 stitches, BRK, knit 1.
Row 2A (RS): With C1, knit 1, *Yf-Sl1-YO, BRK; repeat from * to last 2 stitches, Yf-Sl1-YO, knit 1. Slide stitches back to other end of needle to work another RS row.
Row 2B (RS): With C2, purl 1, *BRP, Yf-Sl1-YOF; repeat from * to last 2 stitches, BRP, purl 1.

Repeat Rows 1A–2B for pattern.

STITCH PATTERN CHOICES (CONT.)
Brioche Stitch with Self Edging
Odd number of stitches; 4-row repeat

This selvedge treatment is more difficult to work (you must take care not to drop the yarn overs on the edge stitches) but is more visually cohesive with the Brioche fabric.

Cast on with C1 (worsted weight), then slide the stitches back to other end of needle so that C1 is hanging at the L edge (you will begin with C2 (fingering weight) at the R edge).

Setup Row (RS): With C2 (fingering weight), *Yf-Sl1-YOF, purl 1; repeat from * to last stitch, Yf-Sl1-YOF.

Row 1A (WS): With C1 (worsted weight), BRP (taking care to hold the first YO in place by anchoring it with your finger as you work this stitch), *Yf-Sl1-YOF, BRP; repeat from * to end, taking care to work the last YO together with its stitch (they will appear separated). Slide stitches back to other end of needle to work another WS row.
Row 1B (WS): With C2, slip first stitch purlwise, YO, *BRK, Yf-Sl1-YO; repeat from * to end.
Row 2A (RS): With C1, BRK (taking care to hold the first YO in place by anchoring it with your finger as you work this stitch), *Yf-Sl1-YO, BRK; repeat from * to end, taking care to work the last YO together with its stitch (they will appear separated). Slide stitches back to other end of needle to work another RS row.
Row 2B (RS): With C2, Yf-Sl1-YOF, *BRP, Yf-Sl1-YOF; repeat from * to end.

Repeat Rows 1A–2B for pattern.

SCARF (WRAP)
TUBULAR CAST ON FOR BRIOCHE
If you do not wish to work a Tubular Cast On, cast on 43 (83) stitches using Size A 32" circular needle (suggested size: 4 mm/ US 6), C1 (Shelter), and a very loose method, then proceed to the "Main Pattern" section of pattern.

With Size B 32" circular needle (suggested size: 3¾ mm/ US 5) and waste yarn, loosely cast on 22 (42) stitches using your preferred method. Do not join.

Foundation Row (WS): With C1 (*Shelter*; worsted weight), purl all stitches in row. This row is worked directly into your waste yarn stitches.
Increase Row (RS): *Knit 1, insert your L needle tip from front to back under the running thread between the stitch you just worked and the next stitch on L needle, then purl this stitch (increasing one); repeat from * to last stitch, knit 1. Upon completion of this row you will have 43 (83) stitches on your needle

You may remove the waste yarn from your tubular edge at any time by carefully snipping it with scissors and unraveling it; however, it is recommended that you wait until you have worked at least 1-2" of fabric before removing. Take care during this process to avoid accidentally cutting any of your working yarn. You may leave your waste yarn in your project through completion of knitting and blocking if you wish. If you choose to leave it in, the waste yarn will protect your tubular edge from being damaged or overstretched during knitting and blocking.

MAIN PATTERN

Slide the stitches back to other end of needle so that C1 is hanging at the L edge (you will begin with C2 at the R edge).

Work in Brioche Stitch (see Stitch Patterns) as follows: work the Setup Row once, then work Rows 1A–2B one hundred and ninety times, then work Row 1A–1B once more.

Work until there are 381 visible rows (762 rows worked) on each face of the fabric. Place locking markers every 10 or 20 rows as you go to aid in counting.
Note: When you count your rows, each visible row equals two rows worked.

Piece measures approximately 63½" from cast-on, but may vary slightly depending on your gauge before blocking. Break C2.

TUBULAR BIND OFF

If you are not using a Tubular Bind Off, bind off all stitches loosely as follows: With C1, BRK, *purl 1, pass second stitch on R needle over first stitch, BRK, pass second stitch on R needle over first stitch; repeat from * to end, fasten off last stitch.

Using current needle and Size B needle, bind off all stitches using the Tubular Bind Off (see Techniques section, p. 129) and C1, with RS facing for dividing stitches. Treat the slipped stitch/yarn over pairs on the front needle each as one stitch.

FINISHING

Block piece following the Wet Blocking (Blocking Wire Method) instructions in the Techniques section (p. 132), stretching to about 10% larger than finished schematic measurements (about 14½ (28)" by 84"). Weave in ends neatly.

TRAVELER COWL

Traveler is a study in movement and texture. The cowl's prominent rope cables are composed of four smaller cable motifs, lending a sense of depth to the finished fabric. The cartridge rib flows directly from the hem into the cable patterns on the cowl body, adding to the piece's overall texture. Camouflaged decreases within the cabled section give the cowl a gentle funnel shape that sits nicely on the neck and shoulders.

SPREAD	SCHEMATIC	PATTERN	CHART
12	42	43	46

TRAVELER

Overview

MATERIALS
440 yards of worsted weight wool yarn
4 skeins of Brooklyn Tweed *Shelter* (100% American Targhee-Columbia wool; 140 yards/50g)
Photographed in color Sweatshirt

GAUGE
25½ stitches & 30 rounds = 4" in pattern from Traveler Chart with Size A needle(s), after blocking
One 35-stitch repeat from Traveler Chart (measured at Rounds 17–44) measures approximately 5½" wide with Size A needle(s), after blocking
25 stitches & 32 rounds = 4" in 2x4 Cartridge Rib with Size B needle(s), after blocking

NEEDLES
Size A (for Main Fabric)
One 24" circular needle in size needed to obtain chart gauge listed
Suggested Size: 5 mm (US 8)
Size B (for Ribbing)
One 24" circular needle, three sizes smaller than Size A or in size needed to obtain rib gauge listed
Suggested Size: 3¾ mm (US 5)

DIMENSIONS
34½" [87.5 cm] circumference at base; 28¾" [73 cm] circumference at top
12" [30.5 cm] height
Measurements taken from relaxed fabric after blocking

TOOLS
Stitch markers (including one in a unique color or style for BOR), two cable needles (CN), T-pins (optional), blunt tapestry needle

SKILL LEVEL
●●○○○
Adventurous Beginner
Knitter's choice of cast on, increasing and decreasing, circular knitting, cable knitting, written and charted instructions provided

TRAVELER

Schematic

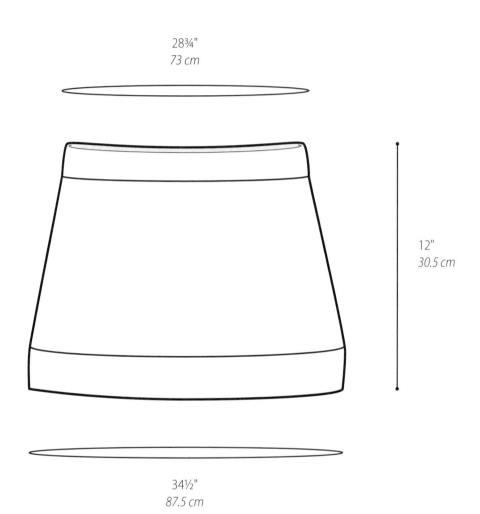

28¾"
73 cm

12"
30.5 cm

34½"
87.5 cm

TRAVELER

Pattern

CONSTRUCTION NOTES
- The cowl is worked circularly from the bottom up.
- The cowl may be worked from either the chart or the written instructions.
- Read all chart rounds from right to left.

STITCH PATTERN
2x4 Cartridge Rib
Multiple of 6 stitches; 2-round repeat

Round 1: *Knit 4, purl 2; repeat from * to end.
Round 2: Purl 1, *knit 2, purl 4; repeat from * to last 5 stitches, knit 2, purl 3.
Repeat Rounds 1 & 2 for pattern.

COWL
With Size B 24" circular needle (suggested size: 3¾ mm/US 5), cast on 216 stitches using the Long-Tail Cast On or another method of your choice. Place unique marker for BOR and join for working in the round, being careful not to twist your ring of stitches.

LOWER RIBBING
Work Rounds 1–16 of Traveler Chart, or work 16 rounds in 2x4 Cartridge Rib (see Stitch Pattern at left).

COWL BODY
Switch to Size A 24" circular needle (suggested size: 5 mm/US 8).

Work Round 17 of chart, placing additional markers after each chart repeat, or follow Round 17 as written below.

Round 17: *Knit 2, SSK, knit 2, k2tog, knit 2, purl 2, knit 4, purl 2, knit 2, M1P, knit 2, p2tog, knit 2, M1P, knit 2, purl 2, knit 4, purl 2, place marker; repeat from * 5 more times, omitting last marker placement (BOR marker is here). [210 stitches now on needle]

Work Rounds 18–80 of chart, or follow written instructions below (see Chart Legend for special abbreviations).

Round 18: *Knit 8, purl 3, knit 2, purl 3, [knit 2, purl 1] 3 times, [knit 2, purl 3] twice, slip marker; repeat from * to end.
Round 19: *Knit 8, purl 2, knit 4, purl 2, [1/1 LC, purl 1] 3 times, 1/1 LC, purl 2, knit 4, purl 2, slip marker; repeat from * to end.
Round 20: Repeat Round 18.
Round 21: *2/2 RC, 2/2 LC, purl 2, knit 4, purl 2, [1/1 LC, purl 1] 3 times, 1/1 LC, purl 2, knit 4, purl 2, slip marker; repeat from * to end.
Rounds 22–24: Repeat Rounds 18–20.
Round 25: *Knit 8, purl 2, knit 4, purl 2, 5/6 LT, purl 2, knit 4, purl 2, slip marker; repeat from * to end.
Rounds 26–30: Repeat Rounds 20–24.
Rounds 31–42: Repeat Rounds 19–30.
Rounds 43 & 44: Repeat Rounds 19 & 20.
Round 45: *2/2 RC, 2/2 LC, purl 2, knit 4, SSP, [1/1 LC, purl 1] 3 times, 1/1 LC, p2tog, knit 4, purl 2, slip marker; repeat from * to end. [198 stitches remain]
Rounds 46: *Knit 8, purl 3, knit 2, purl 2, [knit 2, purl 1] 3 times, knit 2, purl 2, knit 2, purl 3, slip marker; repeat from * to end.
Round 47: *Knit 8, purl 2, knit 4, purl 1, [1/1 LC, purl 1] 4 times, knit 4, purl 2, slip marker; repeat from * to end.
Round 48: Repeat Round 46.
Round 49: *Knit 8, purl 2, knit 4, purl 1, 5/6 LT, purl 1, knit 4, purl 2, slip marker; repeat from * to end.
Round 50: Repeat Round 46.
Round 51: *2/2 RC, 2/2 LC, purl 2, knit 4, purl 1, [1/1 LC, purl 1] 4 times, knit 4, purl 2, slip marker; repeat from * to end.
Rounds 52–54: Repeat Rounds 46–48.
Rounds 55 & 56: Repeat Rounds 47 & 48.
Rounds 57–60: Repeat Rounds 51–54.
Rounds 61 & 62: Repeat Rounds 49 & 50.
Round 63: *2/2 RC, 2/2 LC, SSP, knit 4, purl 1, [1/1 LC, purl 1] 4 times, knit 4, p2tog, slip marker; repeat from * to end. [186 stitches remain]
Round 64: *Knit 8, purl 2, knit 2, purl 2, [knit 2, purl 1] 3 times, [knit 2, purl 2] twice, slip marker; repeat from * to end.
Round 65: *Knit 8, purl 1, knit 4, purl 1, [1/1 LT, purl 1] 4 times, knit 4, purl 1, slip marker; repeat from * to end.
Round 66: Repeat Round 64.
Rounds 67 & 68: Repeat Rounds 65 & 66.
Round 69: *2/2 RC, 2/2 LC, purl 1, knit 4, purl 1, [1/1 LC, purl 1] 4 times, knit 4, purl 1, slip marker; repeat from * to end.
Rounds 70–72: Repeat Rounds 66–68.
Round 73: *Knit 8, purl 1, knit 4, purl 1, 5/6 LT, purl 1, knit 4, purl 1, slip marker; repeat from * to end.
Rounds 74–78: Repeat Rounds 68–72.
Round 79: *Knit 4, purl 1, knit 2, KFB, purl 1, knit 4, purl 1, k2tog, knit 3, p2tog, [knit 4, purl 1] twice, slip marker; repeat from * to end. [180 stitches remain]
Round 80: Purl 1, *knit 2, purl 3; repeat from * to last 4 stitches, knit 2, purl 2.

Piece measures approximately 10½" from cast-on edge.

UPPER RIBBING

Switch to Size B 24" circular needle.

Work Rounds 81–92 of chart or follow written instructions below, removing all markers except for BOR marker on next round.

Round 81: *Knit 4, purl 1; repeat from * to end.
Round 82: Purl 1, *knit 2, purl 3; repeat from * to last 4 stitches, knit 2, purl 2.
Rounds 83–92: Repeat Rounds 81 & 82 five times.

Bind off all stitches in pattern (work as for Round 81 while binding off).

FINISHING

Weave in remaining ends neatly on WS of cowl. Block cowl to schematic measurements following the Wet Blocking instructions in the Techniques section on p. 132.

TRAVELER

Traveler Chart

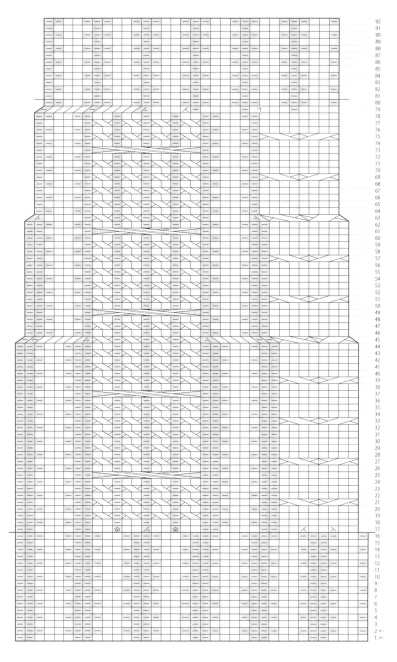

Begins as a 36-stitch repeat; decreases to an 30-stitch repeat

Chart is repeated 6 times per round

TRAVELER

Legend

☐ ***Knit:** Knit stitch

− ***Purl:** Purl stitch

◪ **K2tog:** Knit two stitches together *(1 stitch decreased; leans right)*

◨ **SSK (Modified):** Slip 1 stitch knitwise from L to R needle, replace stitch on L needle in new orientation then knit two stitches together through the back loops *(1 stitch decreased; leans left)*

◨ or ◨ **SSP:** Slip 2 stitches knitwise, one at a time, transfer stitches back to L needle in their new orientation, then purl the stitches together through the back loops *(1 stitch decreased; leans left)*

◪ or ◪ **P2tog:** Purl two stitches together *(1 stitch decreased; leans right)*

⚲ **M1P:** With L needle tip, pick up the running thread between stitch just worked and first stitch on L needle *from back to front*. Purl the running thread through the front loop *(1 stitch increased)*

⊻ **KFB:** Knit into front and then into back of next stitch *(1 stitch increased)*

⋈ **1/1 LC:** Slip 1 stitch to CN and *hold in front*. Knit 1 stitch from L needle. Knit stitch from CN

⋈ ***2/2 LC:** Slip 2 stitches to CN and *hold in front*. Knit 2 stitches from L needle. Knit 2 stitches from CN

⋈ ***2/2 RC:** Slip 2 stitches to CN and *hold in back*. Knit 2 stitches from L needle. Knit 2 stitches from CN

⋈ **5/6 LT:** Slip 5 stitches to first CN and *hold in front*. [1/1 LC, purl 1] twice from L needle. [1/1 LC, purl 1, 1/1 LC] from CN. (Use second CN for working 1/1 LC while stitches are held on first CN)

— **Needle Change:** Indicates position in chart where a change in needle size occurs (see written pattern)

*Symbols marked with an asterisk may appear slanted on some rows in order to maintain the chart's true shape.
Work these symbols as indicated in Legend above

HALO SHAWL

A classic Pi Shawl worked circularly from the center out comes in two sizes and can be further customized to your preferred dimensions. The concentric rings of eyelets adorning the shawl remind me of ripples radiating from a stone cast into still water. With easy stitch patterns and plenty of free rounds of stockinette throughout, Halo offers up a wonderful balance of technical engagement and meditative flow.

SPREAD	SCHEMATIC	PATTERN	CHART
14	50	51	54

HALO

Overview

MATERIALS

1485 (1820) yards of fingering weight wool yarn

6 (7) skeins of Brooklyn Tweed *Loft* (100% American Targhee-Columbia wool; 275 yards/50g)

Photographed in colors Almanac (Small Shawl) & Snowbound (Large Shawl)

GAUGE

17 stitches & 28 rows = 4" in stockinette stitch, after blocking

Note: Due to the Pi Shawl construction method, your finished gauge will vary slightly from one section of the shawl to another once piece is blocked into circular shape.

NEEDLES

One each 16" and 32" circular needles and one set of double-pointed needles (DPNs)* in size needed to obtain gauge listed

Suggested Size: 3¾ mm (US 5)

*32" circular needle can be used instead of DPNs if using the Magic Loop method for working small circumferences in the round (e.g., the center of the shawl).

DIMENSIONS

Small (Large) Shawl

46 (54)" [117 (137.5) cm] diameter (including edging)

Measurements taken from relaxed fabric after lace-blocking

Note that the edgings are the same depth on both shawls, though the larger shawl has an additional repeat. This is due to the distance from the previous Pi Increase Round and the effect of circular blocking.

TOOLS

Stitch marker, T-pins, blunt tapestry needle, crochet hook one or two sizes smaller than gauge needle for working circular cast on

SKILL LEVEL

Intermediate

Circular cast on, increasing and decreasing, lace knitting, charted instructions, knitting in the round, knit-two-together bind off (optional)

HALO

Schematic

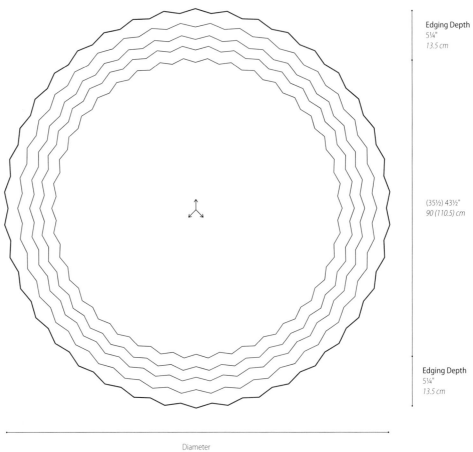

Edging Depth
5¼"
13.5 cm

(35½) 43½"
90 (110.5) cm

Edging Depth
5¼"
13.5 cm

Diameter
46 (54)"
117 (137.5) cm

HALO

Pattern

CONSTRUCTION NOTES

- The shawl is worked from the center out, beginning with a Circular Cast On (see Techniques section, p. 124). It uses traditional Pi Shawl construction (Elizabeth Zimmermann's method) and is shaped using concentric rings of increases. As the diameter of the shawl is doubled, so is the circumference.
- Instructions for the small shawl appear first, with instructions for the large shawl in parentheses. In cases where only one set of instructions appears, it applies to both sizes.
- Read all chart rounds from right to left.
- Some knitters find it easier to use the Magic Loop technique (rather than double-pointed needles) for working small circumferences in the round.
- For best results, use a Felted Join (see Techniques section, p. 126) when joining a new skein of yarn into work. If you are not working with a feltable animal fiber yarn, a Russian Join is recommended. If using the Felted or Russian Join, you will only have two ends to weave in upon completion of your project (the cast-on tail and the bind-off tail).

CUSTOMIZATION NOTES

Though two sizes are provided here, you may easily customize your own finished size with this pattern. Please note that making changes to the finished size and gauge will alter the yarn requirements for the project. If you plan to make a larger shawl, be sure to allow for extra yarn. Keep the following rules and guidelines in mind if you wish to make changes to the pattern:

- Regardless of which ring you are on within the pattern, you will always have a multiple of 12 stitches on your needle(s). The Halo Chart is a multiple of 12 stitches, so you can begin working the edging whenever you like.
- This pattern may be worked in a different yarn weight. For example, you could work the large size in a lace weight yarn or the small size in a DK or worsted weight yarn for a different effect. Choose a needle size slightly larger than you would normally use for your chosen yarn weight.
- Be sure that the number of lace edging rounds you plan to work will fit into the total number of rounds allowed per ring (see bullet points below)—each vertical repeat of the Halo Chart will add 11 rounds.

  - Ring 4 may include a total of 24 rounds before an additional Pi Increase Ring must be worked.
  - Ring 5 may include a total of 48 rounds before an additional Pi Increase Ring must be worked.
  - Ring 6 may include a total of 96 rounds before an additional Pi Increase Ring must be worked.

STITCH PATTERNS

Pi Increase Ring
6-round motif; stitch count doubled after Round 2

Round 1: *Knit 1, YO, knit 1; repeat from * to end.
Round 2: *Knit 1, [knit 1, purl 1] into YO from previous round, knit 1; repeat from * to end.
Round 3: *[YO] twice, SSK, k2tog; repeat from * to end.
Round 4: *[Knit 1, purl 1] into double YO from previous round, knit 2; repeat from * to end.
Round 5: Remove BOR marker, slip 1 stitch from L to R needle, replace marker, *k2tog, [YO] twice, SSK; repeat from * to end.
Round 6: *Knit 1, [knit 1, purl 1] into double YO from previous round, knit 1; repeat from * to end.

Eyelet Ring
6-round motif; no change in stitch count

Round 1: *K2tog, [YO] twice, SSK; repeat from * to end.
Round 2: *Knit 1, [knit 1, purl 1] into double YO from previous round, knit 1; repeat from * to end.
Round 3: *[YO] twice, SSK, K2tog; repeat from * to end.
Round 4: *[Knit 1, purl 1] into double YO from previous round, knit 2; repeat from * to end.
Round 5: Remove BOR marker, slip 1 stitch from L to R needle, replace marker, *k2tog, [YO] twice, SSK; repeat from * to end.
Round 6: *Knit 1, [knit 1, purl 1] into double YO from previous round, knit 1; repeat from * to end.

SHAWL

With DPNs (suggested size: 3¾ mm/US 5), cast on 9 stitches using the Circular Cast On (see Techniques section, p. 124). Divide stitches among DPNs as desired (or use long circular needle for Magic Loop; see Construction Notes), place marker for BOR, and join for working in the round being careful not to twist your ring of stitches.

RING 1
Round 1 (Pi Increase Round): *Knit 1, YO; repeat from * to end. [18 stitches now on needle]
Round 2: *Knit 1, knit 1-tbl into YO from previous round; repeat from * to end.
Note: Knitting the YOs from the previous round through the back loop twists the YO, closing the hole created in the fabric.
Rounds 3 & 4: Knit.

RING 2
Round 1 (Pi Increase Round): *Knit 1, YO; repeat from * to end. [36 stitches now on needle]
Round 2: *Knit 1, knit 1-tbl into YO from previous round; repeat from * to end.
Rounds 3–7: Knit.

RING 3
Rounds 1–6: Work Rounds 1–6 of Pi Increase Ring (see Stitch Patterns). [54 stitches on needle after Round 1; 72 stitches on needle after Round 2]
Rounds 7–13: Knit.

RING 4

Rounds 1–6: Work Rounds 1–6 of Pi Increase Ring.
[108 stitches on needle after Round 1; 144 stitches on needle after Round 2]
Rounds 7–12: Knit.
Rounds 13–18: Work Rounds 1–6 of Eyelet Ring (see Stitch Patterns).
Rounds 19–24: Knit.

RING 5

Rounds 1–6: Work Rounds 1–6 of Pi Increase Ring. [216 stitches on needle after Round 1; 288 stitches on needle after Round 2]
Rounds 7–12: Knit.
Rounds 13–18: Work Rounds 1–6 of Eyelet Ring.
Rounds 19–24: Knit.
Rounds 25–48: Repeat Rounds 13–24 twice.

RING 6 AND EDGING

Rounds 1–6: Work Rounds 1–6 of Pi Increase Ring. [432 stitches on needle after Round 1; 576 stitches on needle after Round 2]
Rounds 7–12: Knit.

Large Shawl Only:
Rounds 13–18: Work Rounds 1–6 of Eyelet Ring.
Rounds 19–24: Knit.
Rounds 25–48: Repeat Rounds 13–24 twice.
Round 49: Knit.

Both Sizes Resume:
Work Rounds 1–11 of Halo Chart 3 (4) times.

Work Rounds 12–15 of chart once.

Bind off all stitches using the Knit-Two-Together Bind Off (see Techniques section, p. 127) or another elastic method of your choice.

Weave in remaining ends invisibly on WS of fabric.

FINISHING

Block shawl to schematic measurements following the *Wet Blocking (Lace-Blocking Method)* instructions in the Techniques section on p. 132.

Halo Chart

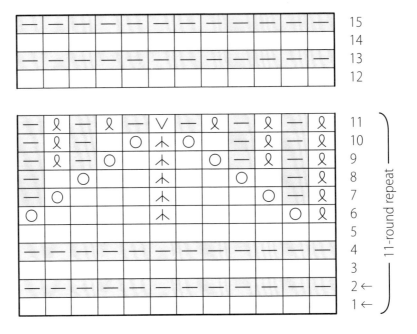

12-stitch repeat

HALO

Legend

☐ **Knit:** Knit stitch

― **Purl:** Purl stitch

◯ **YO (Yarn Over):** With yarn in front, bring yarn over top of R needle from front to back, creating 1 new stitch

⅄ **Raised Central Double Decrease:** Slip 2 stitches from L to R needle at the same time as if to k2tog, knit 1 from L needle, pass the slipped stitches over stitch just worked *(2 stitches decreased)*

∨ **Slip (wyib):** Slip 1 stitch purlwise with yarn in back

ஃ **Knit 1-tbl:** Knit stitch through the back loop, twisting it

FAR HILLS SCARF

A timeless cabled scarf combines classic Aran patterning with subtle texture. Columns of seed stitch flank traditional horseshoe cables to create a beaded effect. (See also the Far Hills Hat on page 86.) A flat cord selvedge — worked using a combination of knit and slipped stitches — flows directly from the top and bottom ribbings, giving a clean and polished finish to this winter wardrobe staple.

SPREAD	SCHEMATIC	PATTERN	CHARTS
16	58	59	61

FAR HILLS SCARF

Overview

MATERIALS

510 (585, 660) yards of worsted weight wool yarn
4 (5, 5) skeins of Brooklyn Tweed *Shelter* (100% American Targhee-Columbia wool; 140 yards/50g)
Medium scarf photographed in color Truffle Hunt

GAUGE

29½ stitches & 29½ rows = 4" in pattern from Cable Chart with Size A needle(s), after blocking
18-stitch center motif from Cable Chart measures 2⅝" wide with Size A needle(s), after blocking

NEEDLES

Size A (for Main Fabric)
One pair of straight needles or a 32" circular needle* in size needed to obtain gauge listed
Suggested Size: 5 mm (US 8)

Size B (for Ribbing)
One 24" long or longer circular needle, three sizes smaller than Size A
Suggested Size: 3¾ mm (US 5)

Size C (optional; for Tubular Cast On only)
One 24" long or longer circular needle, one size smaller than Size B
Suggested Size: 3½ mm (US 4)

*Knitter's preferred style of needle may be used

Note: If you have adjusted the needle size to obtain the correct gauge, it may or may not be necessary to make a matching adjustment to the needle size used for Tubular Cast On, due to variances in individual work. You may wish to test your chosen cast-on method on your swatch.

DIMENSIONS

Short (Medium, Long) Scarf
6½" [16.5 cm] wide; 63¼ (72¾, 82¼)" [160.5 (185, 209) cm] long
Measurements taken from relaxed fabric after blocking

TOOLS

Blunt tapestry needle, two cable needles (CN), T-pins, blocking wires (optional)
If working Tubular Cast On, you will also require smooth waste yarn (sport- or DK-weight cotton, silk, or bamboo yarn) and Size C needle. You may use another cast on if desired, omitting these tools.

SKILL LEVEL

Intermediate
Knitter's choice of cast on, increasing and decreasing, cable knitting, charted instructions
Optional: 2x2 tubular cast on and bind off

FAR HILLS SCARF

Schematic

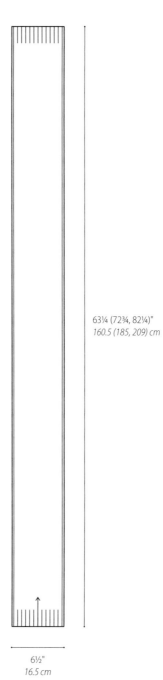

63¼ (72¾, 82¼)"
160.5 (185, 209) cm

6½"
16.5 cm

FAR HILLS SCARF

Pattern

CONSTRUCTION NOTES

- Scarf is worked flat in one piece from end to end.
- Instructions for a Tubular Cast On have been provided in the Techniques section (p. 131). You may substitute a different method if preferred.
- A flat selvedge using a special combination of slipped stitches is worked at each edge throughout the piece.
- Read RS (odd-numbered) chart rows from right to left; read WS (even-numbered) chart rows from left to right.
- The charts have been formatted so that it is easy to alter the length of the scarf in 9½" increments by adding or subtracting 70-row chart repeats.
- Slip all stitches purlwise unless otherwise noted.

SCARF

Tubular Cast On

If you do not wish to work a Tubular Cast On, cast on 42 stitches using Size B circular needle (suggested size: 3¾ mm/US 5) and your preferred method, and proceed to the "Lower Hem" section of pattern.

With Size C circular needle (suggested size: 3½ mm/US 4) and waste yarn, loosely cast on 23 stitches using your preferred method.

Switch to working yarn for Foundation Row, then work Rows 1–6 as directed in Techniques section (p. 131) for Tubular Cast On for Flat Knitting: 2x2 Ribbing with Flat Cord Selvedge. You will have 43 stitches on your needle after Row 1 and 42 stitches on your needle after Row 5.

LOWER HEM

Switch to Size B needle(s) and work Rows 1–22 of Lower Hem Chart, increasing as indicated on Rows 15 and 17, and switching to Size A needle(s) (suggested size: 5 mm/US 8) on Row 19. [48 stitches on needle after Row 17]

MAIN BODY

Note: The two outer cables are crossed every 10th row and the two inner cables are crossed every 14th row. All cables cross on Row 1 of each chart repeat.

Work Rows 1–70 of Cable Chart 6 (7, 8) times (see Construction Notes). Piece measures approximately 60 (69½, 79)" from cast-on edge.

UPPER HEM

Work Rows 1–24 of Upper Hem Chart, switching to Size B circular needle on Row 6, and decreasing as indicated on Rows 7 and 9. [42 stitches remain after Row 9]

If you are not using the Tubular Bind Off, bind off all stitches as follows: K2tog, *work 1 stitch in pattern, pass second stitch on R needle over first stitch; repeat from * to last 2 stitches, slip 2 stitches knitwise at the same time (as if to k2tog), return them to the L needle in new orientation, SSK, pass second stitch on R needle over first stitch, fasten off last stitch.

Tubular Bind Off

Note that this Tubular Bind Off differs slightly from the tutorial in the Techniques section on p. 129.

Setup Row (RS): K2tog, purl 1, slip 1 wyib, purl 2, *knit 2, purl 2; repeat from * to last 4 stitches, slip 1 wyib, purl 1, slip 2 stitches knitwise at the same time (as if to k2tog), return them to the L needle in new orientation, SSK. [40 stitches remain]

Next Row (WS): Purl 1, knit 1, purl 1, knit 2, *purl 2, knit 2; repeat from * to last 3 stitches, purl 1, knit 1, purl 1.

Divide knit and purl stitches (RS facing):

Using current needle and Size C needle, transfer stitches as follows:

Slip first (knit) stitch to front needle, slip 1 purl stitch to back needle, slip 1 knit stitch to front needle, *slip 2 purl stitches to back needle, slip 2 knit stitches to front needle; repeat from * to last 5 stitches, slip 2 purl stitches to back needle, slip 1 knit stitch to front needle, slip 1 purl stitch to back needle, slip last knit stitch to front needle. You now have 20 stitches each on front and back needles.

Graft the stitches from front and back needles together using Kitchener Stitch (see Techniques section, p. 126).

FINISHING

Weave in ends neatly on WS of fabric. Block scarf to schematic measurements following the Wet Blocking (Blocking Wire Method) instructions in the Techniques section on p. 132.

FAR HILLS SCARF

Lower Hem Chart

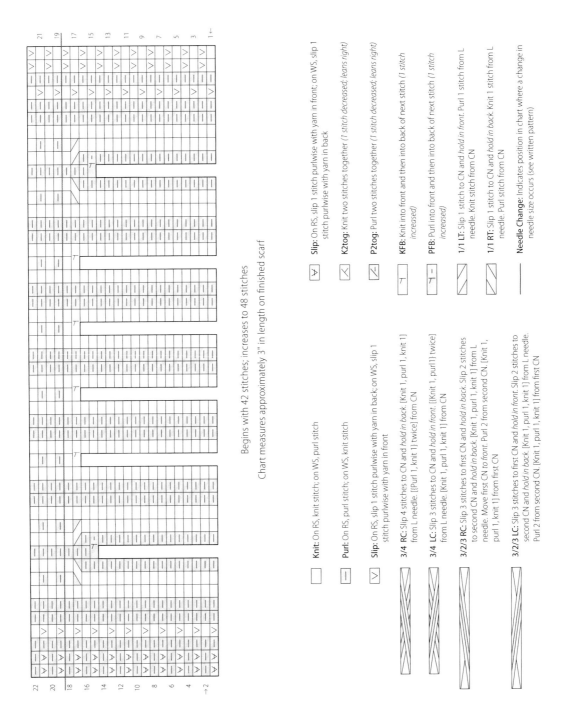

FAR HILLS SCARF

Cable Chart

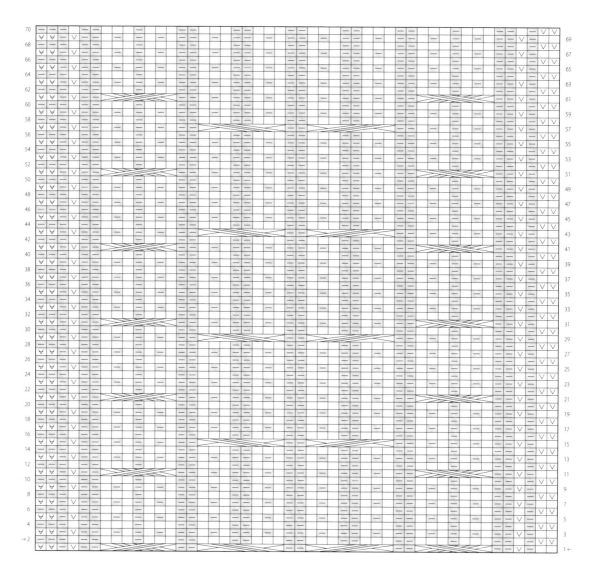

48 stitches; 70-row repeat
Each instance of chart worked will add approximately 9½" to scarf's total length

FAR HILLS SCARF

Upper Hem Chart

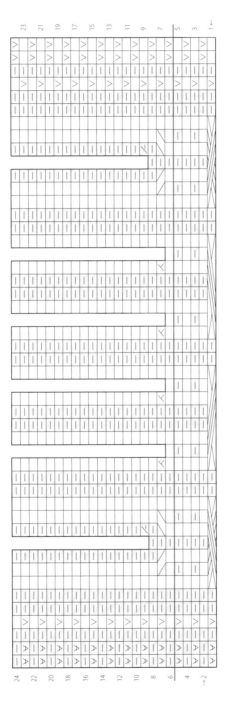

SEEDS HAT

A colorwork hat for knitters who fear colorwork. My goal with Seeds was to capture the Fair Isle look without the fussiness. Only six rounds (eight rounds, if you're knitting the large size) in the hat require the use of two colors, and these rounds alternate color on every stitch to minimize the length of floats and make tensioning a snap. Choose from three sizes, two ribbed brims and a virtually endless combination of colors to make a hat that's uniquely yours.

SPREAD	SCHEMATIC	PATTERN	CHART
18	67	68	71

SEEDS

Overview

MATERIALS

Fingering weight wool yarn in the following approximate amounts:
- 150 (165, 180) yards Color 1 (C1)
- 65 (70, 80) yards Color 2 (C2)
- 30 (35, 40) yards Color 3 (C3)

A pom-pom will require approximately 65 additional yards.

Brooklyn Tweed *Loft* (100% American Targhee-Columbia wool; 275 yards/50g): 1 skein of each color
Photographed in the following colorways:
- Sample I (Upper Left): Nest (C1), Long Johns (C2), & Fossil (C3)
- Sample II (Lower Left): Fossil (C1), Postcard (C2), & Sweatshirt (C3)
- Sample III (Upper Right): Truffle Hunt (C1), Old World (C2), & Faded Quilt (C3)
- Sample IV (Lower Right): Soot (C1), Hayloft (C2), & Woodsmoke (C3)

GAUGE

25 stitches & 35 rounds = 4" in pattern from Seeds Chart with Size A needle(s), after blocking
Please read about Speed-Swatching for Circular Knitting (see Techniques, p. 127).

NEEDLES

Size A (for Main Fabric)
One 16" circular needle and one set of double-pointed needles (DPNs)* in size needed to obtain gauge listed
Suggested Size: 3¾ mm (US 5)

Size B (for Ribbing)
One 16" circular needle*, two sizes smaller than Size A
Suggested Size: 3¼ mm (US 3)

Size C (optional; for Tubular Cast On only)
One 16" circular needle, one size smaller than Size B
Suggested Size: 3 mm (US 2½)

*32" circular needle can be used instead of 16" circular and DPNs if using the Magic Loop method for working small circumferences in the round.

If you have adjusted the needle size to obtain the correct gauge, it may or may not be necessary to make a matching adjustment to the needle size used for Tubular Cast On due to variance in individual work. You may wish to test your chosen cast-on method on your swatch.

SEEDS

Overview (continued)

DIMENSIONS

Small (Medium, Large) to fit teen & adult head circumferences:
19–21 (20–22, 23–24)" [48.5–53.5 (51–56, 58.5–61) cm]
Finished Hat Measurements:
20¼ (21, 22)" [51.5 (53.5, 56) cm] circumference; 8 (8½, 9)" [20.5 (21.5, 23) cm] length
Measurements taken from relaxed fabric after blocking

TOOLS

Stitch markers (including one in a unique style or color for BOR), 2" diameter pom-pom maker (optional; available at craft stores), blunt tapestry needle
If working Tubular Cast On, you will also require smooth waste yarn (fingering weight cotton, silk, or bamboo yarn) and Size C needle. You may use another cast on if desired, omitting these tools. For 2x2 Tubular Cast On, you will also require a cable needle (CN).

●●○○○
SKILL LEVEL

Adventurous Beginner
Knitter's choice of cast on, circular knitting, decreasing, simple chart reading, simple 2-color stranded colorwork, 1x1 or 2x2 tubular cast on instructions provided, pom pom (optional)

SEEDS

Schematic

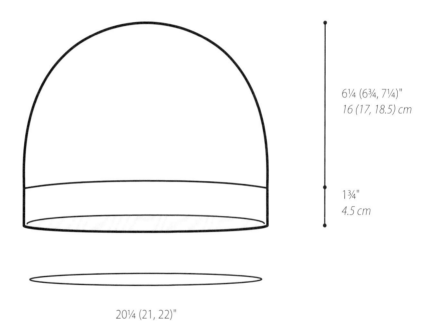

6¼ (6¾, 7¼)"
16 (17, 18.5) cm

1¾"
4.5 cm

20¼ (21, 22)"
51.5 (53.5, 56) cm

SEEDS

Pattern

CONSTRUCTION NOTES

- The hat is worked in the round from the brim to the crown. For the brim, you may choose between 1x1 Ribbing and 2x2 Ribbing.
- While working the chart, if your two-color rounds appear tighter than your single-color rounds, use a slightly larger needle for the two-color rounds only.
- Read about Color Dominance in the Techniques section (p. 125) before beginning. In this chart, on Round 1 the Dominant Color is C2 and the Background Color is C1; on Round 6 the Dominant Color is C3 and the Background Color is C2.
- Read all chart rounds from right to left.

STITCH PATTERNS

1x1 Ribbing
Even number of stitches; 1-round repeat

Round 1: *Knit 1, purl 1; repeat from * to end.
Repeat Round 1 for pattern.

2x2 Ribbing
Multiple of 4 stitches; 1-round repeat

Round 1: *Knit 2, purl 2; repeat from * to end.
Repeat Round 1 for pattern.

HAT

Before beginning, choose either 1x1 or 2x2 Ribbing for the hat brim (see Construction Notes).

BRIM

If you do not wish to work a Tubular Cast On, cast on 124 (128, 136) stitches using Size B 16" circular needle (suggested size: 3¼ mm/US 3), C1, and your preferred method. Place marker and join for working in the round being careful not to twist your ring of stitches, then proceed to the "Work Ribbing" section of piece.

With Size C 16" circular needle (suggested size: 3 mm/US 2½) and waste yarn, loosely cast on 63 (65, 69) stitches using your preferred method.

1x1 Tubular Cast On Only:
Switch to C1 for Foundation Row, then work Row/Rounds 1–4 as directed in Techniques section (p. 129); you will have 124 (128, 136) stitches on your needle(s) after Round 3.

2x2 Tubular Cast On Only:
Switch to C1 for Foundation Row, then work Row/Rounds 1–6 as directed in Techniques section (p. 129); you will have 124 (128, 136) stitches on your needle(s) after Round 3.

Both 1x1 and 2x2 Ribbing:
Switch to Size B 16" circular needle.

Work Ribbing
Begin chosen ribbing pattern (see Stitch Patterns); work even until piece measures 1¾" from cast-on edge.

HAT BODY

Increase Round: *Knit 62 (32, 68), M1; repeat from * 1 (3, 1) more time(s). [126 (132, 138) stitches now on needle]

Switch to Size A 16" circular needle (suggested size: 3¾ mm/US 5) and knit 3 rounds.

Work Rounds 1–10 of Seeds Chart 3 (3, 4) times, carrying colors not in use up the inside until they are required again. Piece measures approximately 5¾ (5¾, 6¾)" from cast-on edge.

CROWN

As you shape the crown, switch to DPNs when necessary for number of stitches in round.

Break C2 and C3; continue in C1 only.

Next Round: *Knit 21 (22, 23), place marker; repeat from * 4 more times, knit 21 (22, 23).

Size Medium Only:
Knit 1 round.
Decrease Round: *Knit to 2 stitches before marker, SSK, slip marker; repeat from * to end. [126 stitches remain]
Knit 2 rounds.

All Sizes Resume:
Crown Decrease Round: *K2tog, knit to 2 stitches before marker, SSK, slip marker; repeat from * to end. (12 stitches decreased)

Repeat the Crown Decrease Round every 3rd round 3 (3, 0) more times, then every other round 3 (3, 7) times, then every round twice. [18 stitches remain]

Decrease Round: *CDD, remove marker; repeat from * 5 more times. [6 stitches remain]

Break yarn, leaving an 8" tail. Thread tail on a tapestry needle and draw strand twice through remaining stitches, twisting yarn in the same direction in which it is plied as you go to give it tensile strength. Pull tightly to secure and fasten off on inside of hat.

FINISHING

Weave in remaining ends neatly on WS of hat. Wet-block hat to schematic measurements (see Techniques section, p. 132).

POM-POM (OPTIONAL)

With pom-pom maker, and working according to package instructions, create 2"-diameter pom-pom (or preferred size) using C2 (or preferred color(s)).

Alternatively, you can make your own pom-pom maker out of stiff cardboard. Draw a 3" diameter circle on the cardboard. Draw a second circle, 1" in diameter, centered inside the first. Draw a wedge, approximately 1" wide, joining the two circles. Cut out shape (will be shaped like a "C"). Cut out a second identical cardboard shape. Hold the two pieces of cardboard together and wind the yarn around them until the center hole is filled. With sharp scissors, cut the yarn around the perimeter of the cardboard shapes, then take a length of yarn and wrap it around the short cut strands, wrapping between the two cardboard shapes. Tie very tightly. Trim pom-pom evenly to 2" diameter.

SEEDS

Seeds Chart

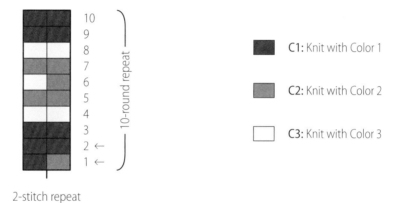

Color Dominance (see Construction Notes):
*On Round 1 the Dominant Color is C2 and the Background Color is C1;
on Round 6 the Dominant Color is C3 and the Background Color is C2*

TESSERA COWL

I discovered this tessellated colorwork motif on a pair of traditional mittens from Latvia. Despite its historic origins, the pattern struck me as quite modern and I loved how the use of three colors allowed for a wider variety of color play than traditional stranded colorwork using only two shades. When choosing colors for your own cowl, try combining a light, medium and dark value in your color scheme to show your work to best effect.

SPREAD	SCHEMATIC	PATTERN	CHART
20	74	75	77

TESSERA

Overview

MATERIALS

Fingering weight wool yarn in the following approximate amounts:
- 535 yards Color 1 (C1)
- 445 yards Color 2 (C2)
- 140 yards Color 3 (C3)

Brooklyn Tweed *Loft* (100% American Targhee-Columbia wool; 275 yards/50g):
- 2 skeins C1
- 2 skeins C2
- 1 skein C3.

Sample 1 photographed in colors Hayloft (C1), Bale (C2), and Fossil (C3).
Sample 2 photographed in colors Old World (C1), Flannel (C2), and Barn Owl (C3).

GAUGE

24 stitches & 28 rounds = 4" in pattern from Tessera Chart with Size A needle, after blocking
Please read about Speed-Swatching for Circular Knitting (see Techniques section, p. 127).

NEEDLES

Size A (for Main Fabric)
One 24" circular needle in size needed to obtain gauge listed
Suggested Size: 4 mm (US 6)

Size B (for Needle Shaping)
One 24" circular needle, one size smaller than Size A
Suggested Size: 3¾ mm (US 5)

Size C (for Needle Shaping)
One 24" circular needle, one size larger than Size A
Suggested Size: 4½ mm (US 7)

DIMENSIONS

13¼" [33.5 cm] height; 28" [71 cm] circumference at center of cowl
Measurements taken from relaxed fabric after blocking

TOOLS

Stitch markers, locking markers, 4½ mm (US 7) crochet hook and smooth waste yarn in a contrasting color for Provisional Cast On, T-pins (optional), blocking wires (optional), 2 blunt tapestry needles

●●●○○
SKILL LEVEL

Intermediate
Provisional cast on, three-color stranded colorwork, circular knitting, charted instructions, grafting

TESSERA

Schematic

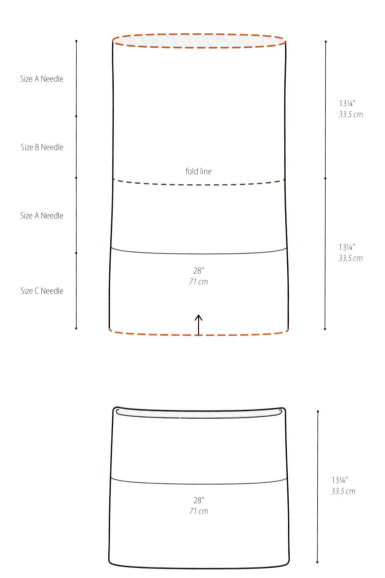

Working View (above) is shown prior to grafting/finishing cowl; orange dashed lines indicate edges that are joined together by grafting. Cowl is shaped subtly by way of changing needle sizes throughout; stitch count does not change. Finished View (below) shows cowl after grafting; final cowl height is 13¼".

TESSERA

Pattern

CONSTRUCTION NOTES

- The cowl is worked circularly, beginning with a Crocheted Provisional Cast On (see Techniques, p.125).
- The cowl has a slight funnel shape created by needle shaping (altering the finished width of the piece by changing the gauge of the fabric). The outer fabric and the inner self-facing are each worked with two different needle sizes: three needle sizes are used altogether. The inner self-facing is worked at a slightly tighter gauge so that it fits nicely inside the outer fabric.
- The live stitches at the end of the cowl are joined to the provisionally cast-on stitches at the beginning using Kitchener Stitch (see Techniques section, p. 126).
- Before you begin, you may wish to review the information regarding Color Dominance in the Techniques section on p. 125.
- Read all chart rounds from right to left.

COWL

OUTER FABRIC

With Size C 24" circular needle (suggested size: 4½ mm/US 7), crochet hook and smooth waste yarn, cast on 168 stitches using the Crocheted Provisional Cast On (see Techniques section, p. 125). Break waste yarn.

Knit 1 row with C2. Without turning piece, place marker for BOR and join for working in the round, being careful not to twist your ring of stitches.

Work Rounds 1–12 of Tessera Chart four times. Place a locking marker in last row worked (this will help you count how many rows have been worked with each size needle).

Switch to Size A 24" circular needle (suggested size: 4 mm/US 6). Work Rounds 1–12 three times. Piece measures approximately 13¼" from cast-on edge. Place a locking marker in last round worked.

INNER SELF-FACING

Switch to Size C 24" circular needle. Work Rounds 1 & 2 once (the cowl will fold at these rounds).

Switch to Size B 24" circular needle (suggested size: 3¾ mm/US 5). Work Rounds 3–12 once, then repeat Rounds 1–12 twice more. Place a locking marker in last round worked.

Switch to Size A 24" circular needle (suggested size: 4 mm/US 6). Work Rounds 1–12 four times. Piece measures approximately 26½" from cast-on edge.

FINISHING

Leave 168 live stitches on Size A 24" circular needle, then carefully undo provisional cast on and transfer the resulting 168 stitches to Size C 24" circular needle.

Thread tapestry needle with a 112" length of C2 and graft stitches on each needle together using Kitchener Stitch (see Techniques section, p. 126).

Weave in remaining ends neatly. Block cowl to schematic measurements following the Wet Blocking instructions in the Techniques section on p. 132.

TESSERA

Tessera Chart

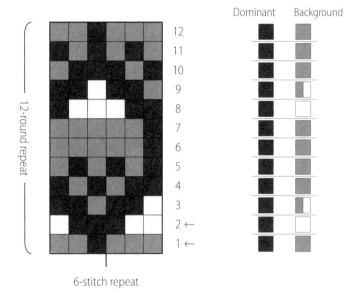

12-round repeat

6-stitch repeat

■ **C1:** Knit with Color 1 (*Dominant Color*)

■ **C2:** Knit with Color 2 (*Background Color*)

□ **C3:** Knit with Color 3 (*Background Color*)

BYWAY SCARF

When it comes to cold-weather wardrobe pieces, the chunky cableknit scarf is my go-to choice for both function and style. Byway can be knit as either a traditional scarf (right) or a dramatic wrap (left) for those who prefer to make a statement with their neckwear. The cable and garter ridge motif that traverses the length of the scarf is mirrored across the vertical axis and punctuated by clean blocks of moss stitch for a pleasing overall composition.

SPREAD	SCHEMATIC	PATTERN	CHARTS
22	80	81	84

BYWAY

Overview

MATERIALS
740 (1185) yards of chunky weight wool yarn
4 (6) skeins of Brooklyn Tweed *Quarry* (100% American Targhee-Columbia wool; 200 yards/100g)
Photographed in colors Serpentine (Scarf) & Moonstone (Wrap)

GAUGE
14 stitches & 24 rows = 4" in Moss Stitch
Measure gauge from relaxed fabric after wet-blocking

NEEDLES
One pair of straight needles or a 32" circular needle* in size needed to obtain gauge listed
Suggested Size: 6½ mm (US 10½)
*Knitter's preferred style of needle may be used

DIMENSIONS
11 (18)" [28 (45.5) cm] wide
80" [203 cm] long
Measurements taken from relaxed fabric after blocking

TOOLS
Cable needle (CN), blunt tapestry needle, T-pins, blocking wires (optional)

SKILL LEVEL
●●○○○
Adventurous Beginner
Knitter's choice of cast on, increasing and decreasing, simple cable knitting, written and charted instructions provided

BYWAY

Schematic

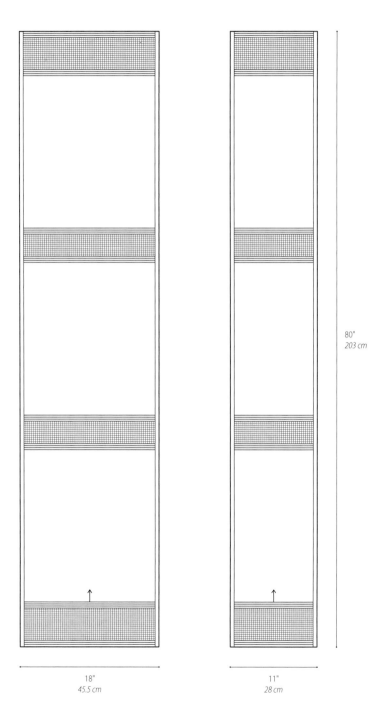

Pattern

CONSTRUCTION NOTES

- Both the scarf and wrap are worked flat in one piece from end to end.
- A flat selvedge using a special combination of slipped stitches is worked at each edge throughout the piece.
- Slip all stitches purlwise unless otherwise indicated.
- Read RS (odd-numbered) chart rows from right to left; read WS (even-numbered) chart rows from left to right.
- Instructions for the scarf appear first, followed by the wrap in parentheses. If only one figure appears, it applies to both items.
- For best results, wet-block piece using blocking wires to straighten edges and square corners (see Techniques section, p. 132).
- When weaving in ends with gently spun yarns, twist the yarn several times in the direction in which it is plied before threading the tapestry needle with the yarn end. Add more twist as you sew, if necessary. You may wish to weave in the ends as you go.
- If working with Brooklyn Tweed Quarry, download a free Tip Card at www.brooklyntweed.com/tips/quarry.

SCARF (WRAP)

With straight or circular needle(s) (suggested size: 6½ mm/ US 10½), cast on 40 (66) stitches using the Long-Tail Cast On or another method of your choice.

MOSS & GARTER BLOCK I

Work Rows 1–18 of Moss and Garter Block Chart, working Rows 8–11 five times, or follow written instructions below.

Row 1 (RS): Knit 2, purl 1, slip 1 wyib, purl 1, knit to last 5 stitches, purl 1, slip 1 wyib, purl 1, slip last 2 stitches to CN, bring yarn to front between CN and R needle, turn CN a half-turn clockwise, and remount the 2 stitches on R needle (these stitches are now in the opposite order).
Row 2 (WS): Knit 3, purl 1, knit to last 4 stitches, purl 1, knit 1, slip 2 wyif.
Row 3: Knit 2, purl 1, slip 1 wyib, purl 1, knit to last 5 stitches, purl 1, slip 1 wyib, purl 1, slip 2 wyif.
Rows 4–7: Repeat Rows 2 & 3 twice.
Row 8: Knit 3, *purl 1, knit 1; repeat from * to last 5 stitches, knit 1, purl 1, knit 1, slip 2 wyif.
Row 9: Knit 2, purl 1, slip 1 wyib, purl 1, *purl 1, knit 1; repeat from * to last 5 stitches, purl 1, slip 1 wyib, purl 1, slip 2 wyif.
Row 10: Knit 3, purl 1, knit 1, *knit 1, purl 1; repeat from * to last 3 stitches, knit 1, slip 2 wyif.
Row 11: Knit 2, purl 1, slip 1 wyib, purl 1, *knit 1, purl 1; repeat from * to last 5 stitches, purl 1, slip 1 wyib, purl 1, slip 2 wyif.
Rows 12–27: Repeat Rows 8–11 four times.
Row 28: Repeat Row 8.
Row 29: Repeat Row 3.
Row 30: Repeat Row 2.
Rows 31–34: Repeat Rows 29 & 30 twice.

CABLE BLOCK I

Work Rows 1–26 of Cable Block Chart, working Rows 5–20 seven times and working repeat sections as indicated, or follow written instructions below.

Row 1 (RS): Knit 2, purl 1, slip 1 wyib, purl 1, {knit 6, [KFB] 3 times, knit 2} 1 (2) time(s), knit 8 (12), {knit 2, [KFB] 3 times, knit 6} 1 (2) time(s), purl 1, slip 1 wyib, purl 1, slip 2 wyif. [46 (78) stitches now on needle(s)]

Row 2 (WS): Knit 3, purl 1, knit 1, [purl 4, knit 2, purl 6, knit 2] 1 (2) time(s), purl 8 (12), [knit 2, purl 6, knit 2, purl 4] 1 (2) time(s), knit 1, purl 1, knit 1, slip 2 wyif.

Row 3: Knit 2, purl 1, slip 1 wyib, purl 1, [knit 4, purl 2, knit 6, purl 2]   1 (2) time(s), knit 8 (12), [purl 2, knit 6, purl 2, knit 4] 1 (2) time(s), purl 1, slip 1 wyib, purl 1, slip 2 wyif.

Row 4: Repeat Row 2.

Row 5: Knit 2, purl 1, slip 1 wyib, purl 1, [knit 4, purl 2, 3/3 RC, purl 2] 1 (2) time(s), knit 8 (12), [purl 2, 3/3 LC, purl 2, knit 4] 1 (2) time(s), purl 1, slip 1 wyib, purl 1, slip 2 wyif.

Row 6: Repeat Row 2.

Row 7: Repeat Row 3.

Row 8: Knit 3, purl 1, knit 1, [knit 6, purl 6, knit 2] 1 (2) time(s), knit 8 (12), [knit 2, purl 6, knit 6] 1 (2) time(s), knit 1, purl 1, knit 1, slip 2 wyif.

Rows 9–12: Repeat Rows 7 & 8 twice.

Row 13: Repeat Row 5.

Row 14: Repeat Row 8.

Row 15: Repeat Row 3.

Row 16: Repeat Row 8.

Rows 17–20: Repeat Rows 3 & 4 twice.

Rows 21–116: Repeat Rows 5–20 six times.

Row 117: Repeat Row 5.

Rows 118–120: Repeat Rows 2–4.

Row 121: Knit 2, purl 1, slip 1 wyib, purl 1, {knit 6, [k2tog] 3 times, knit 2} 1 (2) time(s), knit 8 (12), {knit 2, [k2tog] 3 times, knit 6} 1 (2) time(s), purl 1, slip 1 wyib, purl 1, slip 2 wyif. [40 (66) stitches remain]

Row 122: Knit 3, purl 1, knit to last 4 stitches, purl 1, knit 1, slip 2 wyif.

MOSS & GARTER BLOCK II

Work Rows 3–18 of Moss and Garter Block Chart, working Rows 8–11 three times, or follow written instructions below.

Row 1 (RS): Knit 2, purl 1, slip 1 wyib, purl 1, knit to last 5 stitches, purl 1, slip 1 wyib, purl 1, slip 2 wyif.

Row 2 (WS): Knit 3, purl 1, knit to last 4 stitches, purl 1, knit 1, slip 2 wyif.

Row 3: Repeat Row 1.

Rows 4 & 5: Repeat Rows 2 & 3.

Row 6: Knit 3, *purl 1, knit 1; repeat from * to last 5 stitches, knit 1, purl 1, knit 1, slip 2 wyif.

Row 7: Knit 2, purl 1, slip 1 wyib, purl 1, *purl 1, knit 1; repeat from * to last 5 stitches, purl 1, slip 1 wyib, purl 1, slip 2 wyif.

Row 8: Knit 3, purl 1, knit 1, *knit 1, purl 1; repeat from * to last 3 stitches, knit 1, slip 2 wyif.

Row 9: Knit 2, purl 1, slip 1 wyib, purl 1, *knit 1, purl 1; repeat from * to last 5 stitches, purl 1, slip 1 wyib, purl 1, slip 2 wyif.

Rows 10–17: Repeat Rows 6–9 twice.

Row 18: Repeat Row 6.

Rows 19–24: Repeat Rows 1 & 2 three times.

CABLE BLOCK II
Repeat Cable Block I.

MOSS & GARTER BLOCK III
Repeat Moss and Garter Block II.

CABLE BLOCK III
Repeat Cable Block I.

MOSS & GARTER BLOCK IV
Work Rows 3–18 of Moss and Garter Block Chart, working Rows 8–11 five times, or follow written instructions below.

Rows 1–32: Repeat Rows 3–34 of Moss and Garter Block I.

Bind off knitwise as follows: [K2tog] twice, pass second stitch on R needle over first stitch, *knit 1, pass second stitch on R needle over first stitch; repeat from * to last 4 stitches, SSK, pass second stitch on R needle over first stitch, slip 2 stitches knitwise at the same time (as if to k2tog), return them to the L needle in new orientation, SSK, pass second stitch on R needle over first stitch, fasten off last stitch.

FINISHING
Weave in ends neatly on WS of fabric (see Construction Notes). Block piece to schematic measurements following the Wet Blocking (Blocking Wire Method) instructions in the Techniques section on p. 132.

Moss & Garter Block Chart

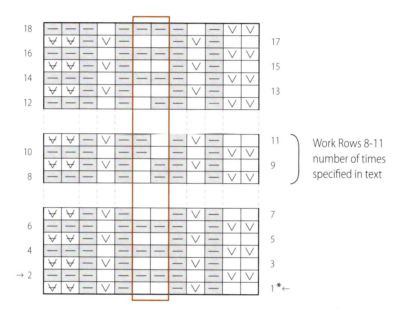

2-stitch repeat

*For Moss & Garter Block I only, see written instructions for special treatment of last two stitches of Row 1

Knit: On RS, knit stitch; on WS, purl stitch

Purl: On RS, purl stitch; on WS, knit stitch

KFB: Knit into front and then into back of next stitch *(1 stitch increased)*

3/3 LC: Slip 3 stitches to CN and *hold in front*. Knit 3 stitches from L needle. Knit 3 stitches from CN

3/3 RC: Slip 3 stitches to CN and *hold in back*. Knit 3 stitches from L needle. Knit 3 stitches from CN

Slip: On RS, slip 1 stitch purlwise with yarn in back; on WS, slip 1 stitch purlwise with yarn in front

Slip: On RS, slip 1 stitch purlwise with yarn in front; on WS, slip 1 stitch purlwise with yarn in back

K2tog: Knit two stitches together *(1 stitch decreased; leans right)*

No Stitch: No stitch exists here in your knitting. This symbol is a tool used to keep the chart aligned properly when the stitch count in a row changes. Ignore this symbol and proceed to next working stitch in row

Repeat: Bracketed motif is repeated more than once

BYWAY

Cable Block Chart

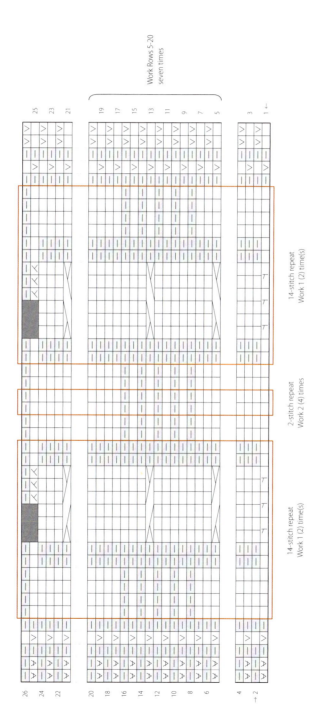

FAR HILLS HAT

This deeply textured beanie uses the same beaded cable found on the Far Hills Scarf (page 56), so you can knit a matched set of accessories. Here the beaded cable is reinterpreted as chains of diminishing horseshoes that encircle the hat as they climb to the crown. Instructions are provided for a tubular cast-on, which gives the finished hat professional polish and a more durable and elastic edge.

SPREAD	SCHEMATIC	PATTERN	CHART
24	88	89	90

FAR HILLS HAT

Overview

MATERIALS

190 yards of worsted weight wool yarn
2 skeins of Brooklyn Tweed *Shelter* (100% American Targhee-Columbia wool; 140 yards/50g)
Photographed in colors Foothills & Artifact

GAUGE

27 stitches & 30 rounds = 4" in Far Hills Hat Chart pattern with Size A needle(s), after blocking
One 18-stitch motif from Far Hills Chart (half of chart, measured at Rounds 1–14) measures approximately 2¾" wide with Size A needle(s), after blocking

NEEDLES

Size A (for Main Fabric)
One 16" circular needle and one set of double-pointed needles (DPNs)* in size needed to obtain gauge listed
Suggested Size: 5 mm (US 8)

Size B (for Ribbing)
One 16" circular needle*, three sizes smaller than Size A
Suggested Size: 3¾ mm (US 5)

Size C (for Tubular Cast On only)
One 16" circular needle*, one size smaller than Size B
Suggested Size: 3½" mm (US 4)

*32" circular needle can be used instead of 16" circular and DPNs if using the Magic Loop method for working small circumferences in the round.

If you have adjusted the needle size to obtain the correct gauge, it may or may not be necessary to make a matching adjustment to the needle size used for Tubular Cast On due to variance in individual work. You may wish to test your chosen cast-on method on your swatch.

DIMENSIONS

21¼" [54 cm] circumference (to comfortably fit average adult head sizes 20–24" [51–61 cm])
8¾" [22.5 cm] length
Measurements taken from relaxed fabric after blocking

TOOLS

Stitch markers, cable needle (CN), blunt tapestry needle
If working Tubular Cast On, you will also require smooth waste yarn (sport- or DK-weight cotton, silk, or bamboo yarn) and Size C needle. You may use another cast on if desired, omitting these tools.

SKILL LEVEL

●●●○○

Intermediate
Knitter's choice of cast on, increasing and decreasing, circular knitting, cable knitting, charted instructions with shaping, optional 2x2 tubular cast on

FAR HILLS HAT

Schematic

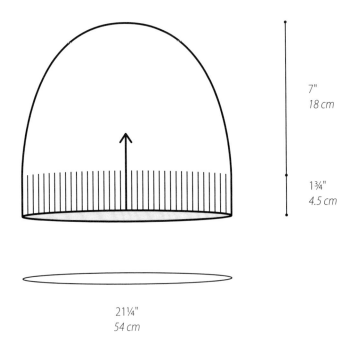

FAR HILLS HAT

Pattern

CONSTRUCTION NOTES
- The hat is worked in the round from the brim to the crown.
- Read all chart rounds from right to left.

STITCH PATTERN
2x2 Ribbing
Multiple of 4 stitches; 1-round repeat

Round 1: *Knit 2, purl 2; repeat from * to end.
Repeat Round 1 for pattern.

HAT
2x2 Tubular Cast On
If you do not wish to work a Tubular Cast On, cast on 112 stitches using Size B 16" circular needle (suggested size: 3¾ mm/US 5), working yarn, and your preferred method. Place marker and join for working in the round being careful not to twist your ring of stitches, then proceed to the "Work Ribbing" section of piece.

With Size C 16" circular needle (suggested size: 3½ mm/US 4) and waste yarn, loosely cast on 57 stitches using your preferred method.

Switch to working yarn for Foundation Row, then work Row/Rounds 1–6 as directed in Techniques section on p. 129; you will have 112 stitches on your needle(s) after Round 3.

Switch to Size B 16" circular needle.

Work Ribbing
Begin 2x2 Ribbing (see Stitch Pattern); work even until piece measures 1¾" from cast-on edge.

HAT BODY
Switch to Size A 16" circular needle (suggested: 5 mm/US 8).

Increase Round: *[Knit 3, M1] 7 times, knit 4, M1, knit 3; repeat from * 3 more times. [144 stitches now on needle]

Work Rounds 1–14 of Far Hills Hat Chart, working chart 4 times per round. Piece measures approximately 3¾" from cast-on edge.

CROWN
Switch to DPNs when necessary for number of stitches in round.
Work Rounds 15–51 of chart, working decreases as charted. [32 stitches remain after Round 47]

Break yarn, leaving a 10" tail. Thread tail on a tapestry needle, twist yarn a few times in the direction in which it is plied, and draw strand twice through remaining stitches. Pull tightly to secure and fasten off on inside of hat.

FINISHING
Weave in remaining ends neatly on WS of hat. Block hat to schematic measurements following the Wet Blocking (Hat Method) instructions in the Techniques section on p. 132.

FAR HILLS HAT

Far Hills Hat Chart

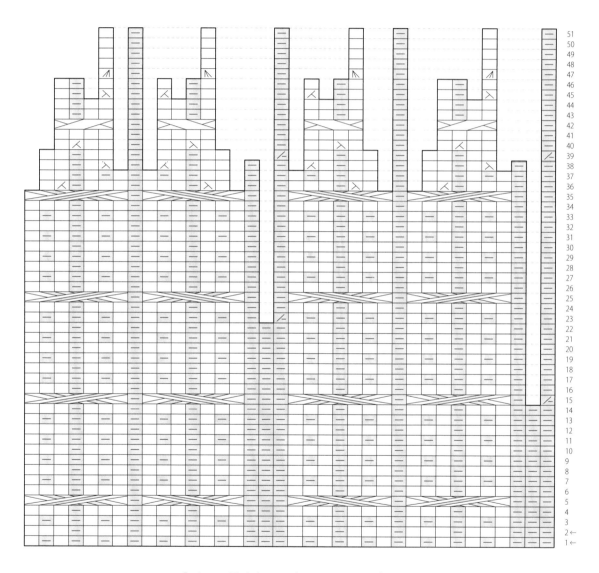

Begins as a 36-stitch repeat; decreases to an 8-stitch repeat

Chart is repeated 4 times per round

FAR HILLS HAT

Legend

☐ **Knit:** Knit stitch

⊟ **Purl:** Purl stitch

◪ **K2tog:** Knit two stitches together *(1 stitch decreased; leans right)*

◩ **SSK (Modified):** Slip 1 stitch knitwise from L to R needle, replace stitch on L needle in new orientation then knit two stitches together through the back loops *(1 stitch decreased; leans left)*

◪ **P2tog:** Purl two stitches together *(1 stitch decreased; leans right)*

◪ **K3tog:** Knit three stitches together *(2 stitches decreased; leans right)*

◩ **SSSK:** Slip 1 stitch knitwise from L to R needle, replace stitch on L needle in new orientation then knit three stitches together through the back loops *(2 stitches decreased; leans left)*

2/2 LC: Slip 2 stitches to CN and *hold in front*. Knit 2 stitches from L needle. Knit 2 stitches from CN

2/2 RC: Slip 2 stitches to CN and *hold in back*. Knit 2 stitches from L needle. Knit 2 stitches from CN

3/4 RC: Slip 4 stitches to CN and *hold in back*. [Knit 1, purl 1, knit 1] from L needle. [{Purl 1, knit 1} twice] from CN

3/4 LC: Slip 3 stitches to CN and *hold in front*. [{Knit 1, purl1} twice] from L needle. [Knit 1, purl 1, knit 1] from CN

REDSHIFT SHAWL

Here's a bold project that will keep you on your knitting toes. Redshift's graphic herringbone fabric makes a statement with bright, high-contrast colors as shown; pair quieter shades, though, and it assumes a subtle and sophisticated air. The shawl's unusual construction (which includes both circular and flat knitting, thanks to the help of steeks) makes for adventurous knitting that may teach you a few new tricks along the way.

SPREAD	SCHEMATIC	PATTERN	CHART
26	94	95	99

REDSHIFT

Overview

MATERIALS

975 yards Color 1 (C1) + 535 yards Color 2 (C2) of fingering weight wool yarn
Brooklyn Tweed *Loft* (100% American Targhee-Columbia wool; 275 yards/50g): 4 skeins C1 and 2 skeins C2. Photographed in colors Cinnabar (C1) and Woodsmoke (C2)

GAUGE

26 stitches & 26 rounds = 4" in colorwork pattern from chart with Size A needle(s), after blocking
26 stitches & 52 rows (26 ridges) = 4" in garter stitch with Size B needle(s), after blocking
Be sure to swatch for both gauges. The correct proportion of the shawl depends upon achieving a square gauge (same number of stitches and rounds/garter ridges in a given measurement). Please read about Speed-Swatching for Circular Knitting (see Techniques section, p. 127).

NEEDLES

Size A (for Colorwork Fabric)
One each 24" and 32" circular needles and one set of double-pointed needles (DPNs)* in size needed to obtain chart gauge listed
Suggested Size: 4 mm (US 6)
Size B (for Garter Stitch Edging)
Two 32" circular needles in size needed to obtain garter stitch gauge listed
Suggested Size: 3¾ mm (US 5)
*32" circular needle can be used instead of DPNs if using the Magic Loop method for working small circumferences in the round (e.g. the end of the shawl).
Due to variance between knitters, your colorwork fabric should be swatched prior to knitting your shawl to determine whether or not this needle size should be larger, smaller or equal to the size used for the edging.

DIMENSIONS

Approximately 63½" [161.5 cm] wingspan; 30" [76 cm] height at center spine
Measurements taken from relaxed fabric after blocking

TOOLS

Stitch markers (including one in a unique style or color for BOR), 3¾ mm (US F-5) crochet hook and smooth waste yarn for Provisional Cast On, T-pins (optional), blocking wires (optional), blunt tapestry needle, sewing needle and thread to match C1 (optional)
You will need either of the following options to secure the steeks: a sewing needle and thread to match C1; or a 3¾ mm (F-5) and a 3½ mm (US E-4) crochet hook and a small amount of C1 (see Construction Notes).

SKILL LEVEL

Advanced
Provisional cast on, two-color stranded colorwork, steeks (crochet or sewn method), charted instructions, picking up stitches, circular knitting

REDSHIFT

Schematic

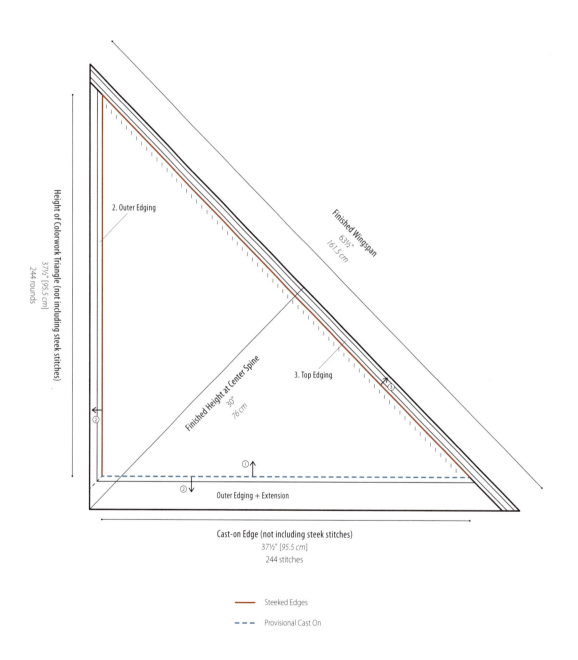

REDSHIFT

Pattern

CONSTRUCTION NOTES

- The shawl is worked circularly from a Provisional Cast On to one point, with a steek. The steek is then secured and cut open. Stitches are picked up along the straight edge of the triangle, and the stitches of the provisional cast on are released. The edging for these two sides is worked in one piece in garter stitch. The edging for the third side is picked up along the decreased edge of the triangle and along the side edges of the previous edging piece, and also worked in garter stitch.
- Familiarize yourself with Color Dominance in the Techniques section (p. 125) before beginning. In this pattern, the Dominant Color is always C1 and the Background Color is always C2.
- Read all chart rounds from right to left.
- The steek edges will be visible from the WS of the shawl. Be sure to secure the steeks with matching thread if you are sewing the steek or matching yarn if you are crocheting the steek. Do not machine-sew the steek because the space that remains near the top of the shawl will not be sufficient to maneuver it into the sewing machine. If working a crocheted steek, note that the facing will be slightly bulkier than a hand-sewn steek.
- When binding off edging stitches, use a larger needle if necessary to achieve a tidy yet elastic edge.
- For best results, wet-block shawl using blocking wires as described in the Techniques section (p. 132).

SHAWL

With Size A 32" circular needle (suggested size: 4 mm/US 6), crochet hook and smooth waste yarn, cast on 244 stitches using the Crocheted Provisional Cast On as directed in Techniques section (p. 125). Break waste yarn. Join C1 and purl 1 row.

Row 1 (RS): Work Row 1 of Redshift Chart to end, place marker for steek, using the Backward Loop Cast On (see Techniques section, p. 124), [cast on 1 stitch with C2, cast on 1 stitch with C1] 7 times, cast on 1 stitch with C2, place marker for BOR, join for working in the round, being careful not to twist your ring of stitches. [244 shawl stitches + 15 steek stitches]

Work Rounds 2–4 once. [241 shawl stitches remain + 15 steek stitches]

Work Rounds 5–24 eleven times, changing to 24" circular needle and then to DPNs when necessary for number of stitches in round. [21 shawl stitches remain + 15 steek stitches]

Work Rounds 25–44 once. [1 shawl stitch remains + 15 steek stitches]

Bind off remaining stitches.

Preliminary Finishing

With sewing needle and thread or crochet hook, sew or crochet steek and carefully cut it open along the center of the steek (see Techniques section, p. 128). If crocheting the steek, use the larger hook to work along the slanted edge (the hypotenuse) of the triangle, and the smaller hook to work along the straight edge of the triangle. Steam-block the triangle to 37½" by 37½" by 53" as directed in Techniques section (p. 128), not including the steeks.

OUTER EDGING

With one Size B 32" circular needle (suggested size: 3¾ mm/ US 5), C2 and RS facing, begin at bound-off edge of shawl and pick up and knit 244 stitches along straight side edge of shawl (working between last shawl stitch and first steek stitch), M1-BL, place marker, carefully undo Provisional Cast On and transfer the resulting 243 stitches to second Size B needle as they are released, then knit across them with first needle. Set second needle aside. Do not join; work back and forth in rows. [488 stitches now on needle]

Setup Row (WS): Knit.

Increase Row (RS): Knit 1, KFB, knit to 1 stitch before marker, KFB, slip marker, KFB, knit to last 2 stitches, KFB, knit 1. (4 stitches increased)
Next Row (WS): Knit.

Repeat the last 2 rows once more. Break C2. [496 stitches now on needle]

Switch to C1, then repeat the last 2 rows 4 more times. Do not break C1. [512 stitches now on needle]

Transfer the 256 stitches along the cast-on edge of shawl to the second Size B 32" circular needle. Remove marker.

EDGING EXTENSION

Join a new ball of C1 at the corner. Work will continue over the 256 stitches on the second needle along the cast-on edge of shawl only.

Increase Row (RS): Knit to last 2 stitches, KFB, knit 1. (1 stitch increased)
Next Row (WS): Knit.

Repeat the last 2 rows 11 more times. Break yarn leaving an 8" tail. [268 stitches now on second needle]

Rejoin Sides

Return to first needle, ready to resume working over held stitches with attached C1.

Increase Row (RS): Knit 1, KFB, knit to end of first needle, pick up and knit 13 stitches (1 stitch in each garter ridge) along side of edging extension, M1-BL, place marker, working across stitches from second needle, KFB, knit to last 2 stitches, KFB, knit 1. Set second needle aside. [541 stitches now on first needle]

Bind off all stitches knitwise from the WS, with a relaxed tension (see Construction Notes).

HYPOTENUSE EDGING

With one Size B 32" circular needle, C1, and RS facing, begin at corner of edging applied to cast-on edge of shawl and pick up and knit 20 stitches (1 stitch in each garter ridge) along side of edging, 324 stitches evenly along sloped side edge of shawl (working between last steek stitch and first shawl stitch and picking up approximately 4 stitches for every 3 rows), and 8 stitches (1 stitch in each garter ridge) along side of edging applied to straight edge of shawl. [352 stitches now on needle]

Setup Row (WS): Knit 18, [M1-BL, knit 16] 19 times, M1-BL, knit 30. [372 stitches now on needle]

Increase Row (RS): Knit 1, KFB, knit to last 2 stitches, KFB, knit 1. (2 stitches increased)
Next Row (WS): Knit.

Break C1. Switch to C2, then repeat the last 2 rows 4 more times. [382 stitches now on needle]

Break C2. Switch to C1, then repeat the last 2 rows once more. Work the RS row once again. [386 stitches now on needle]

Bind off all stitches knitwise from the WS, with a relaxed tension.

FINISHING

Weave in ends neatly on WS of fabric. Trim cut steek edges to about ½" wide and neatly tack them down to WS using sewing needle and matching thread, taking care to make the corner tidy.

Block shawl to schematic measurements following the Wet Blocking (Blocking Wire Method) instructions in the Techniques section on p. 132.

LEGEND

■ **C1:** Knit with Color 1 (dominant color)

□ **C2:** Knit with Color 2 (background color)

⋀ **K2tog:** Knit two stitches together using color indicated *(1 stitch decreased; leans right)*

□ **Pattern Repeat**

REDSHIFT

Redshift Chart

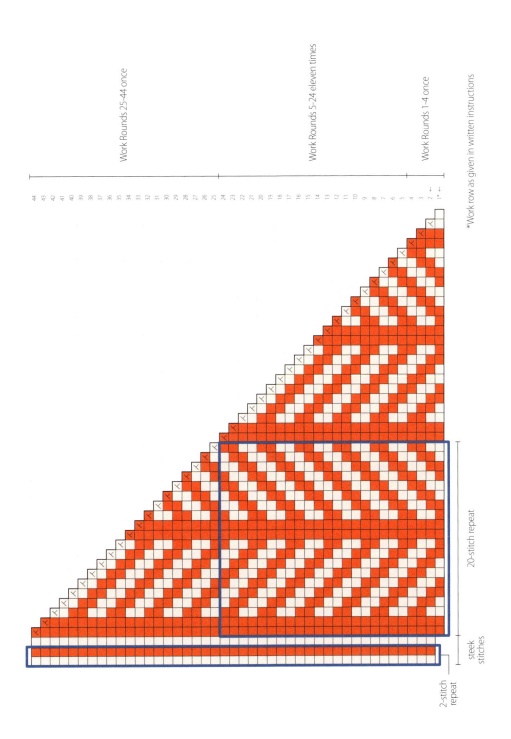

FURROW COWL

This oversized cowl is all about warmth and coziness. Knit to 18" in length, Furrow's cable and moss stitch fabric drapes and folds to garland your neck. Stitches are decreased within the wedge-shaped fields of moss stitch as you work to create a slightly bell-shaped piece that's wider at the base and sits closer to the neck for better insulation. The cowl can easily be shortened if less volume is desired or your yarn quantity is limited.

SPREAD	SCHEMATIC	PATTERN	CHART
28	102	103	105

FURROW COWL

Overview

MATERIALS

480 yards of worsted weight wool yarn
4 skeins of Brooklyn Tweed *Shelter* (100% American Targhee-Columbia wool; 140 yards/50g)
Photographed in colors Tartan and Fossil

GAUGE

18 stitches & 28 rows/rounds = 4" in Moss Stitch with Size A needle(s), after blocking
One 8-stitch motif from Furrow Chart measures 1¼" wide with Size A needle(s), after blocking

NEEDLES

Size A (for Main Fabric)
One 24" circular needle in size needed to obtain chart gauge listed
Suggested Size: 5 mm (US 8)
Size B (for Edging)
One 24" circular needle, three sizes smaller than Size A
Suggested Size: 3¾ mm (US 5)

DIMENSIONS

36¾" [93.5 cm] circumference at base
26¼" [66.5 cm] circumference at top
18" [45.5 cm] height
Measurements taken from relaxed fabric after blocking

TOOLS

Stitch markers (including one in a unique color or style for BOR), cable needle (CN), T-pins (optional), blunt tapestry needle

SKILL LEVEL

Adventurous Beginner
Knitter's choice of cast on, simple cables, circular knitting, increasing and decreasing, written and charted instructions provided

FURROW COWL

Schematic

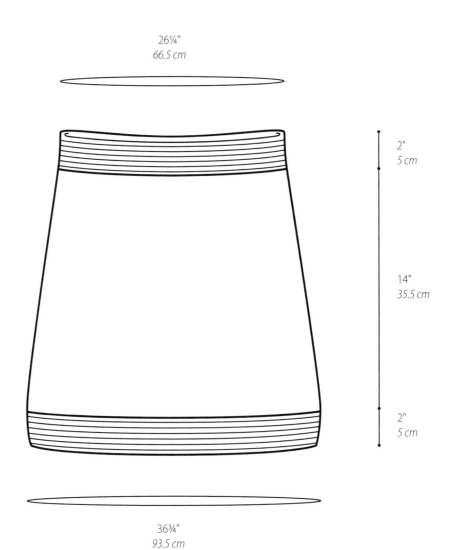

FURROW COWL

Pattern

CONSTRUCTION NOTES
- The cowl is worked circularly from the bottom up.
- The Furrow motif may be worked from either the chart or the written instructions.
- Read all chart rounds from right to left.

STITCH PATTERNS

Moss Stitch
Even number of stitches; 4-round repeat

Rounds 1 & 2: *Purl 1, knit 1; repeat from * to end.
Rounds 3 & 4: *Knit 1, purl 1; repeat from * to end.
Repeat Rounds 1–4 for pattern.

Furrow Motif
Panel of 8 stitches; 6-round repeat

Round 1: Knit 2, purl 4, knit 2.
Round 2: Knit 8.
Round 3: 2/2 LC-purl, 2/2 RC-purl.
Rounds 4–6: Repeat Round 1.
Repeat Rounds 1–6 for panel.

COWL

LOWER EDGING

With Size B 24" circular needle (suggested size: 3¾ mm/ US 5), cast on 168 stitches using the Cabled Cast On (see Techniques section, p. 124) or another method of your choice. Place unique marker for BOR and join for working in the round, being careful not to twist your ring of stitches.

Next Round: Purl.
Next Round: Knit.

Repeat the last 2 rounds 8 more times, or work until piece measures 2" from cast-on edge ending with a knit round.

COWL BODY

Switch to Size A 24" circular needle (suggested size: 5 mm/ US 8).

Setup Round: *Purl 1, knit 2, [PFB] twice, knit 2, purl 1, place marker, work Round 1 of Moss Stitch (see Stitch Patterns on previous page) over 20 stitches, place marker; repeat from * 5 more times (omitting last marker placement—BOR marker is here). [180 stitches now on needle]

Next Round: *Purl 1, knit 2, purl 4, knit 2, purl 1, slip marker, work Round 2 of Moss Stitch to marker, slip marker; repeat from * 5 more times.

Next Round: *Purl 1, work Round 1 of Furrow Motif (see Stitch Patterns or Chart), purl 1, slip marker, work in Moss Stitch to marker, slip marker; repeat from * 5 more times.

Work 5 rounds even in established stitch patterns.

Decrease Round: *Work as established to marker, slip marker, p2tog (or k2tog to keep in pattern), work in Moss Stitch to 2 stitches before marker, SSK (or SSP to keep in pattern), slip marker; repeat from * 5 more times. (12 stitches decreased)

Repeat the Decrease Round every 28th round 3 more times.

Upon completion of this section, you will have worked the Decrease Round a total of 4 times; you now have 132 stitches on your needle.

Work 5 rounds even in established patterns.

UPPER EDGING

Switch to Size B needle.

Decrease Round: *Knit 3, [k2tog] twice, knit 8, k2tog, knit 5, slip marker; repeat from * 5 more times. [114 stitches remain]

Next Round: Purl, removing all markers except BOR marker.
Next Round: Knit.

Repeat the last 2 rounds 7 more times, then purl 1 more round, or continue as established until edging measures 2", ending with a purl round.

Bind off all stitches knitwise.

FINISHING

Weave in ends neatly on WS of cowl. Wet-block cowl to schematic measurements (see Techniques section, p. 132).

FURROW COWL

Furrow Chart

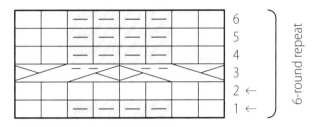

8-stitch panel

	Knit: Knit stitch
—	Purl: Purl stitch
	2/2 LC-purl: Slip 2 stitches to CN and *hold in front*. Knit 2 stitches from L needle. Purl 2 stitches from CN
	2/2 RC-purl: Slip 2 stitches to CN and *hold in back*. Purl 2 stitches from L needle. Knit 2 stitches from CN

FURROW HAT

Here's a fun hat recipe that lets you make four different design decisions to create 16 possible variations from a single pattern. Directions are given for both worsted (Version I) and chunky-weight (Version II) yarn. Choose between a beanie or slouchy fit, a split or circular brim, and include or omit a top loop. This adaptable pattern is great for using up yarn leftovers and making the perfect tailored topper for everyone in the family.

SPREAD	SCHEMATIC	PATTERN	CHARTS
30	109	111	114

FURROW HAT

Overview

MATERIALS

Version I — Worsted Weight:
Beanie (Slouchy)
150 (180) yards of worsted weight wool yarn
2 skeins of Brooklyn Tweed *Shelter* (100% American Targhee-Columbia wool; 140 yards/50g)
Photographed in color Woodsmoke (Beanie; upper right) and Long Johns (Slouchy; lower right)

Version II — Chunky Weight:
Beanie (Slouchy)
115 (155) yards of chunky weight wool yarn
1 skein of Brooklyn Tweed *Quarry* (100% American Targhee-Columbia wool; 200 yards/100g)
Photographed in color Flint (Beanie; upper left) and Hematite (Slouchy; lower left)

GAUGE

Version I — Worsted Weight:
20 stitches & 32 rows = 4" in Moss Stitch with Size A needle(s) and Shelter, after blocking
10-stitch cable motif from chart measures 1¼" wide with Size A needle(s) and Shelter, after blocking

Version II — Chunky Weight:
15 stitches & 24 rows = 4" in Moss Stitch with Size A needle(s) and Quarry, after blocking
10-stitch cable motif from chart measures 2" wide with Size A needle(s) and Quarry, after blocking

NEEDLES

Version I — Worsted Weight:
Size A (for Main Fabric)
One 16" circular needle and one set of double-pointed needles (DPNs)* in size needed to obtain gauge listed
Suggested Size: 4½ mm (US 7)
Size B (for Brim)
One 16" circular needle* two sizes smaller than Size A
Suggested Size: 3¾ mm (US 5)

FURROW HAT

Overview

NEEDLES

Version II — Chunky Weight:
Size A (for Main Fabric)
One 16" circular needle and one set of double-pointed needles (DPNs)* in size needed to obtain gauge listed
Suggested Size: 6 mm (US 10)
Size B (for Brim)
One 16" circular needle* two sizes smaller than Size A
Suggested Size: 5 mm (US 8)
*32" circular needle can be used instead of 16" circular and DPNs if using the Magic Loop method for working small circumferences in the round.

DIMENSIONS

Version I — Worsted Weight:
20¾" [52.5 cm] circumference (to comfortably fit average adult head sizes 20–24" [51–61 cm]); Beanie length 7½" [19 cm]; Slouchy length 9" [23 cm]

Version II — Chunky Weight:
19¾" [50 cm] circumference (to comfortably fit average adult head sizes 20–24" [51–61 cm]); Beanie length 8¼" [21 cm]; Slouchy length 9¼" [23.5 cm]

TOOLS

Stitch markers (including one in a unique color or style for BOR), removable marker or safety pin (if working split brim option only), cable needle (CN), T-pins (optional), blunt tapestry needle
Optional for top loop: 3¾ mm/US F-5 (5 mm/US H-8) crochet hook

SKILL LEVEL

●●●○○

Intermediate
Knitter's choice of cast on, circular knitting, increasing and decreasing, charted instructions, simple cables, simple crochet techniques (chain, slip stitch; optional)

FURROW HAT

Schematics

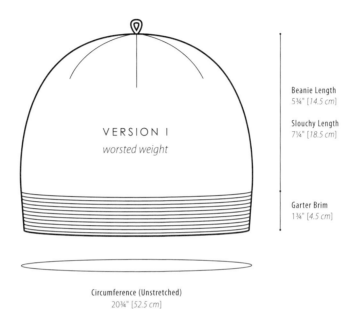

Beanie Length
5¾" [14.5 cm]

Slouchy Length
7¼" [18.5 cm]

Garter Brim
1¾" [4.5 cm]

VERSION I
worsted weight

Circumference (Unstretched)
20¾" [52.5 cm]

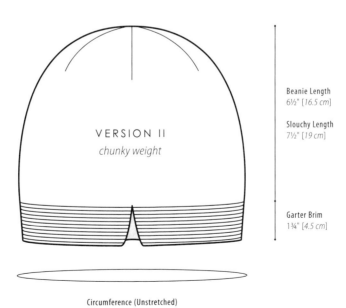

Beanie Length
6½" [16.5 cm]

Slouchy Length
7½" [19 cm]

Garter Brim
1¾" [4.5 cm]

VERSION II
chunky weight

Circumference (Unstretched)
19¾" [50 cm]

FURROW HAT

Design Options

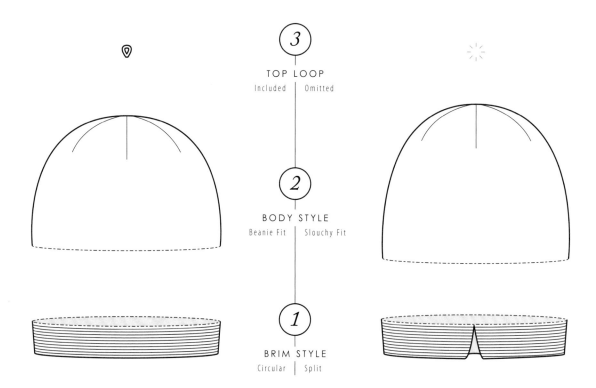

Personalize Your Hat

This pattern provides several design options, allowing you to create a hat that suits your personal style. Choose between a circular or split brim (1), a beanie or slouchy fit (2), the addition of a top loop (3), and worsted or chunky weight yarn (4).

Mix and match these elements to create up to 16 unique styles for yourself or friends and family.

FURROW HAT

Pattern

CONSTRUCTION NOTES

- This pattern includes instructions for both worsted and chunky weight yarns.
- You may choose between a split brim (worked flat) and a circular brim. The hat is worked in the round from the top of the brim to the crown. An optional top loop, worked with a crochet hook, is perfect if you plan to hang your hat on a hook or peg.
- Version I is worked in worsted weight yarn; Version II is worked in chunky weight yarn. Instructions for Version I appear first, with instructions for Version II in parentheses. Where only one set of instructions appears, it applies to both versions.
- Read all chart rounds from right to left. There are different charts for Versions I and II.
- When weaving in ends with gently spun yarns, twist the yarn several times in the direction in which it is plied before threading the tapestry needle with the yarn end. Add more twist as you sew, if necessary. You may wish to weave in the ends as you go.
- If working with Brooklyn Tweed Quarry, download a free Tip Card at www.brooklyntweed.com/tips/quarry.

HAT

BRIM

Follow the instructions below for your preferred brim style — you may choose to work a circular or split brim:

For Circular Brim Only:
With Size B 16" circular needle, cast on 102 (68) stitches using the Cabled Cast On (see Techniques section, p. 124) or another method of your choice. Place a unique marker for BOR and join for working in the round, being careful not to twist your ring of stitches.

Round 1: Purl.
Round 2: Knit.

Repeat the last 2 rounds until piece measures approximately 1¾" from cast-on edge, ending with Round 1 [you will have approximately 9 (7) garter ridges].

Setup Round 1: *Knit 12, KFB, knit 4, place marker; repeat from * to end of round, omitting last marker placement (BOR marker is here). [108 (72) stitches now on needle; 6 (4) sections of 18 stitches each]

Setup Round 2: *Purl 1, Inv-L, purl 1, PFB, purl 1, Inv-R, [purl 1, knit 1] 6 times; repeat from * to end. [126 (84) stitches now on needle; 6 (4) sections of 21 stitches each]

Setup Round 3: *Purl 1, knit 2, purl 4, knit 2, [purl 1, knit 1] 6 times; repeat from * to end.

For Split Brim Only:
With Size B 16" circular needle, cast on 104 (70) stitches using the Long-Tail Cast On or another method of your choice.

You may wish to place a safety pin or removable marker to indicate the RS of your fabric to keep track of your rows in the following section.

Row 1 (RS): Slip 1 wyif, bring yarn to back, knit to end.
Row 2 (WS): Slip 1 wyif, bring yarn to back, knit to end.

Repeat the last 2 rows until piece measures approximately 1¾" from cast-on edge, ending with a WS Row [you will have approximately 9 (7) garter ridges].

Setup Round 1 (RS; work joined in the round): Slip 1 wyif, slip 1 wyib, knit 10, KFB, knit 5, *knit 11, KFB, knit 5; repeat from * 3 (1) more time(s), knit 11, KFB, knit 4, slip 1 wyib, transfer last stitch of row to CN and hold in back. Join work in the round but do not place BOR marker yet. Slip first stitch of row to same CN and hold in back. Now the first stitch of the row is on the L side of CN and the last stitch of the row is on R side of CN. Rotate CN one half-turn (180 degrees) counterclockwise, reversing the position of the stitches. Slip the left-most stitch of CN to L needle and the right-most stitch from CN to R needle. Insert L needle tip purlwise through the first 2 stitches on R needle and knit these 2 stitches together through the back loops. Place unique marker to indicate BOR. [109 (73) stitches now on needle]
Setup Round 2: P2tog, purl 1, Inv-R, [purl 1, knit 1] 6 times, place marker, *purl 1, Inv-L, purl 1, PFB, purl 1, Inv-R, [purl 1, knit 1] 6 times, place marker; repeat from * to last 3 stitches, purl 1, Inv-L, PFB. [126 (84) stitches now on needle]
Setup Round 3: *Purl 2, knit 2, [purl 1, knit 1] 6 times, slip marker, *purl 1, knit 2, purl 4, knit 2, [purl 1, knit 1] 6 times; repeat from * 4 (2) more times, slip 5 stitches purlwise, remove BOR marker, return 5 slipped stitches back to L needle, replace marker for new BOR.

Both Brims Resume:
HAT BODY
You will now work the Hat Body for your chosen Version — switch to Size A 16" circular needle as you proceed.

Version I Only:
Work Rounds 1–23 of Version I Chart for Beanie length or Rounds 1–35 for Slouchy length.

Version II Only:
Work Rounds 1–20 of Version II: Body Chart for both Beanie and Slouchy lengths.

CROWN
Switch to DPNs when necessary for decreasing number of stitches in round.

Version I Only:
Work Rounds 36–55 of Version I Chart for both Beanie and Slouchy lengths. [12 stitches remain]

Version II Only:
Work Rounds Rounds 21–36 of Version II: Beanie Crown Chart or 21–42 of Version II: Slouchy Crown Chart, according to your chosen length. [8 stitches remain]

Both Versions Resume:
Break yarn, leaving a 10" tail. Thread tail on a tapestry needle (see Construction Notes) and draw strand twice through remaining stitches. Pull gently to secure and fasten off on inside of hat.

TOP LOOP (OPTIONAL)

Make a slipknot and place on crochet hook. Join to top of crown using a slip stitch. Work a crocheted chain approximately 2" long.

Version I Only:
Turn work, skip first chain, then work a slip stitch into each chain, ending at crown.

Both Versions Resume:
Break yarn leaving an 8" tail and fasten off. Fold crocheted loop in half and pull end through center top of hat to WS. Secure end of loop to inside of hat.

FINISHING

Weave in remaining ends neatly on WS of hat (see Construction Notes). Block hat to schematic measurements following the Wet Blocking (Hat Method) instructions in the Techniques section on p. 132.

Chunky version with beanie fit, split brim and no top loop

FURROW HAT

Version I Chart (Worsted)

Both Beanie and Slouchy body styles are represented on this chart.
Review written instructions before working.

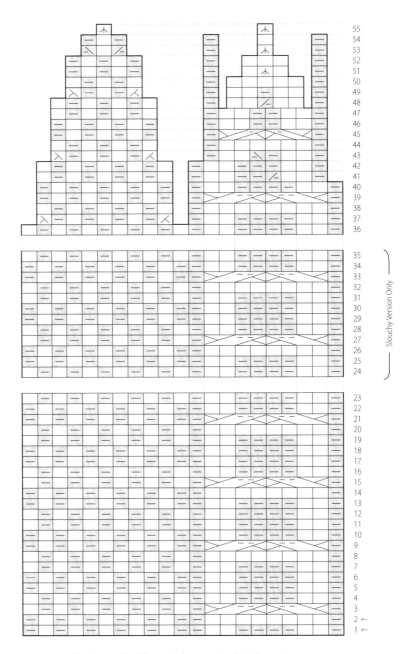

Begins as a 21-stitch repeat, decreases to a 2-stitch repeat;
worked 6 times per round

FURROW HAT

Legend

- **Knit:** Knit stitch
- **Purl:** Purl stitch
- **1/2 LC-purl:** Slip 1 stitch to CN and *hold in front*. Knit 2 stitches from L needle. Purl stitch from CN
- **1/2 RC-purl:** Slip 2 stitches to CN and *hold in back*. Purl 1 stitch from L needle. Knit 2 stitches from CN
- **2/2 LC-purl:** Slip 2 stitches to CN and *hold in front*. Knit 2 stitches from L needle. Purl 2 stitches from CN
- **2/2 RC-purl:** Slip 2 stitches to CN and *hold in back*. Purl 2 stitches from L needle. Knit 2 stitches from CN

- **K2tog:** Knit two stitches together *(1 stitch decreased; leans right)*
- **SSK (Modified):** Slip 1 stitch knitwise from L to R needle, replace stitch on L needle in new orientation then knit two stitches together through the back loops *(1 stitch decreased; leans left)*
- **P2tog:** Purl two stitches together *(1 stitch decreased; leans right)*
- **SSP:** Slip 2 stitches knitwise, one at a time, transfer stitches back to L needle in their new orientation, then purl the stitches together through the back loops *(1 stitch decreased; leans left)*
- **Raised Central Double Decrease:** Slip 2 stitches from L to R needle at the same time as if to k2tog, knit 1 from L needle, pass the slipped stitches over stitch just worked *(2 stitches decreased)*

Worsted version with slouchy fit, circular brim and no top loop

Version II Body Chart (Chunky)

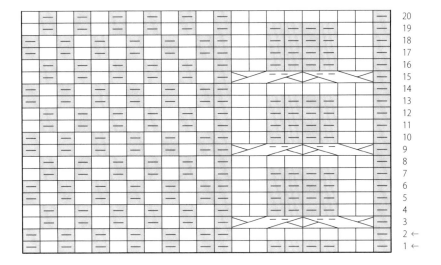

21-stitch repeat;
worked 4 times per round

FURROW HAT

Version II Crown Charts (Chunky)

Work the crown chart that corresponds to your chosen body style (beanie or slouchy)

BEANIE

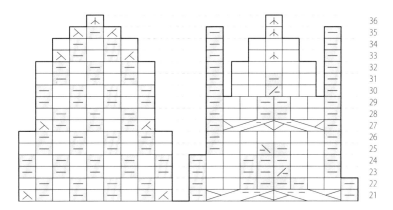

Begins as a 21-stitch repeat, decreases to a 2-stitch repeat;
worked 4 times per round

SLOUCHY

Begins as a 21-stitch repeat, decreases to a 2-stitch repeat;
worked 4 times per round

JOURNAL

A gallery of photos taken during the making of *Woolens*

TECHNIQUES *and* ABBREVIATIONS

TECHNIQUES

BACKWARD LOOP CAST ON — Make a slip knot on R needle to begin. Holding the needle with the slip knot in your right hand, *use the working yarn to make a loop around your left thumb, then place this loop onto the R needle; repeat from * until you have the required number of stitches on your needle. If using this method to cast on stitches to a piece in progress, omit slip knot and begin at *.

CABLED CAST ON — Make a slip knot on L needle to begin, insert R needle into slip knot and knit a new stitch. Place new stitch on L needle. *Insert R needle between the first and second stitch on the L needle, wrap strand of yarn around R needle as you would for a knit stitch and pull through, place this new loop onto L needle; repeat from * until required number of stitches have been cast on. After last stitch has been cast on, slip last stitch purlwise to R needle, bring working yarn to front between needles, return last stitch to L needle and pull working yarn snugly. Repositioning the working yarn in this way creates a cleaner edge at the end of your cast-on row. (If using this method to cast on stitches to a piece in progress, omit the slipknot and begin at *.)

CIRCULAR CAST ON — This circular cast on is a variation of the Emily Ocker circular beginning. Leaving a short tail of 8", form a loop approximately 2" in diameter with yarn crossing at left side of loop, ball end on top of tail end. Pinch yarn crossing between L thumb and middle finger. (Tail trails down from left side of loop (like a lowercase "p") and ball end trails up from left side of loop (like a lowercase "b").)

As you work steps 1 & 2, keep loop loose; once cast on has been completed, the loop may be cinched close by pulling gently on the tail. One repeat of steps 1 & 2 results in one finished stitch on hook.

Step 1: With crochet hook in R hand, insert hook through center of loop from front to back, YO hook with ball end and pull hook up and out through loop. You may wish to secure the ball end over your extended L index finger to make this movement easier. (1 preliminary stitch on hook)
Step 2: With crochet hook positioned at top of loop and hook tip pointing to the left, YO hook with ball end and pull hook through preliminary stitch. (1 finished stitch on hook)

Repeat steps 1 & 2 until you have cast on the required number of stitches. Distribute the stitches equally across multiple DPNs (or long circular needle, if using the Magic Loop method). After working several rounds of pattern, return to the cast on and, gripping the tail as near to

TECHNIQUES

the center loop as possible, gently pull to close the loop. Take care to not pull too hard; you may wish to first twist the CO tail in the direction in which the yarn is plied to give the tail more tensile strength before pulling.

COLOR DOMINANCE

When working stranded fabric with 2 colors, one color will always be more prominent (the Dominant Color), while the other recedes to the background (the Background Color). This effect is controlled by how the yarns are held (when working the one-color in each hand method), or more accurately, how the yarns are floating along the WS. If both yarns are held in the same hand, the effect is controlled by which yarn is stranded above, and which below.

The Dominant Color is held in the left hand, and/or strands below the Background Color on the WS of the fabric. The Background Color is held in the right hand and/or strands above the Dominant Color on the WS of the fabric. Be consistent with how you hold the yarns while working the chart to achieve best results.

CROCHETED PROVISIONAL CAST ON

With waste yarn and crochet hook, make a slipknot and place it on the crochet hook. Crochet 5 or 6 chains before picking up your knitting needle. Holding the crochet hook in your right hand and the knitting needle in your left hand, bring the yarn behind the knitting needle, and with crochet hook held in front of knitting needle, catch the yarn with the crochet hook and draw the loop through the loop that you previously placed on the hook. There is now one loop on your crochet hook and one stitch on your knitting needle. *Bring yarn to back, behind the knitting needle, keeping the crochet hook in front of the knitting needle. Catch a loop of yarn with the hook and draw it through the loop on hook (one new stitch has been cast on to the knitting needle and one new chain made with hook); repeat from * until the desired number of stitches have been cast on to your needle. Note that as you work, the number of stitches will increase on your knitting needle, though you should never have more than one chain on your crochet hook. You now have the desired number of stitches on your needle and one chain on the crochet hook. Chain a few more stitches with the hook (do not catch the knitting needle when making these), then break the yarn leaving a 6" tail and draw tail through last chain. Switch to the working yarn and begin piece as instructed in pattern.

When you are ready to return to these stitches and work in the other direction, undo the chain where it was fastened off and carefully pull out the waste yarn, thus "unzipping" the stitches. Transfer these stitches to your knitting needle as they are unfastened.

TECHNIQUES

FELTED JOIN

This is a method of joining a new ball of yarn without having any ends to weave in. The yarn must be feltable; that is, it should be 100% animal fiber and should not be superwash-treated. This is generally used on reversible projects where there are few good places to hide the ends in seams or on the WS of the work. The following tutorial assumes you are working with a two-ply yarn.

Unravel the plies for the last 3-4" of the old ball of yarn and the first 3-4" of the new ball of yarn. Twist the unraveled plies of both yarn ends together and add a bit of moisture (a few drops of water should be sufficient). Rub the strands together vigorously between your hands, applying heat and friction to felt the plies together. For yarns with three plies or more, you may choose to remove a ply from each unraveled end before felting to reduce bulk.

KITCHENER STITCH (GRAFTING)

This technique is used to sew live stitches together in a way that mimics a row of knitting. Pieces to be joined are live on needles, with RSs facing out and both needle tips pointing to the right. Use a length of yarn approximately 4 times the length of the finished seam, attached to the R edge of the piece (use the yarn the piece was knitted with, or attach a new length of yarn). Thread the yarn onto a blunt tapestry needle and follow the instructions below, working from right to left:

Note: Work into each stitch twice, and treat each slipped stitch/yarn over pair on the Front Needle as one stitch, working into both at once with the tapestry needle.

Step 1: Insert tapestry needle into first stitch on Front Needle as if to purl; pull yarn through, but do not slip this stitch from needle.
Step 2: Insert tapestry needle into first stitch on Back Needle as if to knit; pull yarn through, but do not slip this stitch from needle.
Step 3: Insert tapestry needle into first stitch on Front Needle as if to knit, slipping this stitch off the needle. Insert tapestry needle into next stitch on Front Needle as if to purl and pull yarn through this stitch, tugging it gently.
Step 4: Insert tapestry needle into first stitch on Back Needle as if to purl, slipping this stitch off the needle. Insert tapestry needle into next stitch on Back Needle as if to knit and pull yarn through this stitch, tugging it gently.

TECHNIQUES

Repeat steps 3 & 4 until 2 stitches remain on Front Needle and 1 stitch remains on back needle, adjusting the tension of the sewing yarn every few stitches so that it mimics the tension of the knitting. Repeat step 3 once more (1 stitch remains on each needle). To finish, insert tapestry needle into final stitch on Back Needle as if to purl, slipping it off of needle. Now, insert tapestry needle into final stitch on Front Needle as if to knit, slipping it off of needle. Pull the yarn through and fasten off gently so as not to distort the stitches.

KNIT-TWO-TOGETHER BIND OFF

Knit the first stitch on L needle, then knit the second stitch on L needle, *insert L needle into the 2 stitches on R needle and knit them together (1 stitch on R needle), knit next stitch on L needle; repeat from * until no stitches remain on L needle (1 stitch on R needle). Break yarn and fasten off remaining stitch.

SPEED-SWATCHING FOR CIRCULAR KNITTING

This technique is used to work a gauge swatch for projects knit in the round. When trying to match gauge for a pattern that is knit circularly, it is best to swatch in-the-round as well. Follow the instructions below for "speed-swatching" for circular knitting projects:

Step 1: Using the dominant color (C1 in this pattern) and a circular needle in an appropriate size needle for your target gauge, cast on the total number of stitches for your swatch – including 4 extra selvedge stitches (2 at each side of fabric) that will not be part of your motif. Working yarn is now coming from left side of work.

Step 2: Slide stitches across circular needle from L to R, so stitches are ready to be worked again with RS facing. Bring working yarn across back of work—leaving a very relaxed float—and work the first 2 stitches of the row with the dominant color and background color held together. Now work across row in colorwork pattern to last 2 stitches. Work the last 2 stitches with both yarns held together.

Step 3: Repeat step 2 for every row of swatch worked. Note that the first and last 2 stitches are always worked with both yarns held together. This serves to anchor both of your working yarns at either end of your swatch every row.

Step 4: After completion of all colorwork rows in swatch, bind off stitches with a single color.

Step 5: Cut the long floats at the back of your work down the center. Swatch can now be blocked flat, but will give you an accurate gauge reading for circular knitting. Note that you will have "fringe" on both sides of your swatch; this fringe can be cleaned up by trimming it to 2" in length on each side.

TECHNIQUES

STEAM BLOCKING

Lay finished project flat on an appropriate blocking surface, smoothing fabric flat with your hands. Pin garment or item to instructed dimensions (see Schematic), using T-pins if necessary. Set your iron to the wool setting (medium temperature with steam) and prepare a press cloth (a flat cotton or linen tea towel or piece of cloth of similar weight) by soaking it in water and wringing it out. Lay the damp cloth over the knitted piece and hold the iron about ½" above the cloth, sending bursts of steam through the cloth. The damp cloth will add extra steam and prevent you from accidentally scorching the piece. Re-wet the cloth as needed. Move the cloth and steam each section of the knitting. Allow to dry completely before unpinning.

STEEKING (CROCHET & SEWN METHODS)

Steeks form a "bridge," so that a piece can be knit in the round even when future openings are being constructed (such as armholes, necklines, etc). This is particularly useful when doing colorwork, as it avoids the need to purl back while stranding and makes your work much easier. The steek is reinforced by either crocheting or sewing lines of closely spaced stitches, and then it is cut open.

Securing a Steek: Crochet Method
Note: Secure the steek between the second and third stitches, and between the thirteenth and fourteenth stitches, leaving plenty of space in the center for cutting the steek.

Crocheted steeks must be worked with a feltable (non-superwash) wool yarn. Use a hook slightly smaller than knitting needle size used. The line of single crochets should not pucker or bloat along the edge – if it looks distorted you must change hook size (or try a thinner yarn). Mark the center stitch of the steek. You will be working up the left side (as you face the garment) of the steek, working into the R leg of the left-adjacent stitch and the L leg of the center stitch. When you are at the top of the steek, you will fasten off that yarn, and rejoin new yarn to work down the right side of the steek. For the right side, you will be working into the L leg of the right-adjacent stitch and the R leg of the center stitch. If you crochet left-handed, you will work up the right side and then down the left side.

With crochet hook and matching yarn, beginning at bottom of steek (first round of knitting) and working upwards on one side (between thirteenth and fourteenth stitches), make a slip-knot on hook, *insert hook into R leg of fourteenth stitch and L leg of thirteenth stitch, yarn over hook and draw new loop through both stitch legs (2 loops on hook), then draw new loop through first loop (1 loop remains on hook); repeat from * to top of steek, working into each stitch above the last. Fasten off yarn.

TECHNIQUES

Work down the right side of steek in the same manner, working into the stitch legs between the second and third stitches as described above. Cut steek down center, taking care not to cut any of the yarn used for crocheting.

Securing a Steek: Hand-Sewn Method
Sewn steeks can be used on any type of yarn. Mark the center of the steek. With needle and thread, sew 2 lines of closely spaced stitches down each side of center of steek (4 lines of stitches altogether). Cut steek down center.

TUBULAR BIND OFF:
1X1 RIBBING

This is a method of binding off which uses Kitchener Stitch to create a smooth edge.

Separate the knit and purl stitches (knit stitches are slipped stitch/yarn over pairs) from each other onto 2 separate needles, i.e., *slip the next knit stitch onto Needle 1 (Front), slip the next purl stitch onto Needle 2 (Back); repeat from * until all stitches are separated, with the knit stitches all on the Front Needle and the purl stitches all on the Back Needle.
Proceed as for Kitchener Stitch (p. 126) to bind off the stitches by grafting them together.

TUBULAR CAST ON FOR CIRCULAR KNITTING:
1X1 AND 2X2 RIBBING
Worked over a multiple of 4 stitches

Using Size C needle (as directed in pattern) in preferred style for working in the round, waste yarn, and your preferred cast-on method, loosely cast on the number of stitches directed for piece.

Foundation Row (WS): With working yarn, purl all stitches in row. This row is worked directly into your waste yarn stitches.
Row 1 (Increase Row; RS): *Knit 1, insert your L needle tip from front to back under the running thread between the stitch you just worked and the next stitch on L needle, then purl this stitch (increasing one); repeat from * to last stitch, slip 1 purlwise.

Join your work into the round, being careful not to twist your ring of stitches. Slip the last stitch of your round purlwise from R to L needle, then place a unique marker for BOR. Your stitches will now be arranged such that the round begins with a pair of knit stitches and ends with a purl stitch.

Round 2 (Tubular Purl Round): Slip 2 purlwise with yarn in back, *bring yarn to front, purl 1, bring yarn to back, slip 1 purlwise; repeat from * to end.

Round 3 (Tubular Knit Round): K2tog, *bring yarn to front, slip 1 purlwise, bring yarn to back, knit 1; repeat from * to last stitch, bring yarn to front, slip 1 purlwise. (1 stitch decreased)
Round 4 (Tubular Purl Round): *Bring yarn to back, slip 1 purlwise, bring yarn to front, purl 1; repeat from * to end.

Work following section for 2x2 Ribbing Only:

Up to this point, your stitches have been worked in a 1x1 ribbing arrangement. Before working the next row, you will rearrange the stitches on the needle into a 2x2 ribbing arrangement. You will not use your working yarn when you do the rearrangement. You may use a cable needle (CN) to make the rearranging of stitches easier if you wish. Note that all stitches in this section are slipped purlwise.

Rearrange Stitches for 2x2 Ribbing (RS facing; Non-working): *Slip 1 (a knit stitch) from L to R needle, slip next stitch (a purl stitch) onto CN and hold in back, slip 1 (a knit stitch) from L to R needle, slip 1 from CN to R needle, slip 1 (a purl stitch) from L to R needle; repeat from * to end. You are now back at the BOR, with working yarn ready to be picked up again.
Round 5 (Tubular Knit Round): Resuming with working yarn, *bring yarn to back, knit 2, bring yarn to front, slip 2 purlwise; repeat from * to end.
Round 6 (Tubular Purl Round): *Bring yarn to back, slip 2 purlwise, bring yarn to front, purl 2; repeat from * to end.

For Both 1x1 and 2x2 Ribbing:

You have now completed your tubular rows and will begin working the ribbing. You may remove the waste yarn from your tubular edge at any time by carefully snipping it with scissors and unraveling it; however, it is recommended that you wait until you have worked 1–2" of fabric before removing. Take care during this process to avoid accidentally cutting any of your working yarn.

TECHNIQUES

TUBULAR CAST ON FOR FLAT KNITTING: 2X2 RIBBING WITH FLAT CORD SELVEDGE

Using Size C circular needle (as directed in pattern), waste yarn, and your preferred cast-on method, loosely cast on the number of stitches directed for piece. Do not join.

Foundation Row (WS): Using working yarn, purl all stitches in row. This row is worked directly into your waste yarn stitches.

Row 1 (Increase Row; RS): Knit 1, [Inc + K2tog]†, *insert your L needle tip from front to back under the running thread between the stitch you just worked and the next stitch on L needle, then purl this stitch (increasing one), knit 1; repeat from * to last stitch, [Inc + K2tog]†. Slip last 2 stitches to CN, bring yarn to front between CN and R needle, turn CN a half-turn clockwise, and remount the 2 stitches on R needle (these stitches are now in the opposite order).

Row 2 (Tubular Row; WS): Knit 3, *bring yarn to front, slip 1, bring yarn to back, knit 1; repeat from * to last 2 stitches, bring yarn to front, slip 2.

Row 3 (Tubular Row; RS): Knit 2, *bring yarn to front, slip 1, bring yarn to back, knit 1; repeat from * to last 3 stitches, bring yarn to front, slip 3.

Row 4 (Tubular Row; WS): Repeat Row 2.

Up to this point, your stitches have been worked in a 1x1 ribbing arrangement (with 2-stitch slipped selvedges at either side). Before working the next row, you will rearrange your stitches into a special combination of 2x2 Rib and slipped stitches which aligns with the chart. You will not use your working yarn when you do the rearrangement. You may use a cable needle (CN) to make the rearranging of stitches easier if you wish. Note that all stitches in this section are slipped purlwise.

Rearrange Stitches for 2x2 Ribbing (RS facing; Non-working): Slip 5, *slip next stitch (a knit stitch) onto CN and hold in front, slip 1 (a purl stitch) from L to R needle, slip 1 from CN to R needle, slip 2 stitches (1 knit stitch, 1 purl stitch) from L to R needle; repeat from * to last 6 stitches, slip next stitch (a knit stitch) onto CN and hold in front, slip 1 (a purl stitch) from L to R needle, slip 1 from CN to R needle, slip 4. Now slide your row of stitches across your circular needle so that your working yarn is once again on the L needle, ready to work a RS row.

† [Inc + K2tog]: Pick up the running thread between stitch just worked and the next stitch on L needle and place on L needle, then knit it together with next stitch on L needle. You have picked up a stitch and then decreased it immediately to produce a secure edge on the selvedge of Tubular Cast On.

TECHNIQUES

Row 5 (Tubular Row; RS): Resuming with working yarn, knit 2, bring yarn to front, slip 1, bring yarn to back, knit 1, *bring yarn to front, slip 2, bring yarn to back, knit 2; repeat from * to last 7 stitches, bring yarn to front, slip 2, bring yarn to back, k2tog, bring yarn to front, slip 3. (1 stitch decreased)

Row 6 (Tubular Row; WS): Knit 3, bring yarn to front, slip 1, *bring yarn to back, knit 2, bring yarn to front, slip 2; repeat from * to last 6 stitches, bring yarn to back, knit 2, bring yarn to front, slip 1, bring yarn to back, knit 1, bring yarn to front, slip 2.

You may remove the waste yarn from your tubular edge at any time by carefully snipping it with scissors and unraveling it; however, it is recommended that you wait until you have worked 1–2" of fabric before removing. Take care during this process to avoid accidentally cutting any of your working yarn. You may leave your waste yarn in your project through completion of knitting and blocking if you wish. If you choose to leave it in, the waste yarn will protect your tubular edge from being damaged or overstretched during knitting and blocking.

WET BLOCKING

Fill a sink or basin with warm water and a small amount of delicate dish soap or rinseless wool wash. Submerge fabric in water, gently squeezing out any air bubbles so that the piece can remain under water without being held there. Soak work for 30 minutes, allowing fabric to become completely saturated.

Drain the sink and remove work. If you have used dish soap (rather than rinseless wool wash), you will want to fill the sink again once or twice to rinse the soap from your fabric. Never place knitting directly under running water.

Squeeze out excess water from your work, taking care not to twist or wring fabric. Roll your fabric between two clean bath towels "burrito style" and firmly press towel roll. This will aid in removing moisture from the knitted piece. Remove piece from towels – your fabric should now feel damp but not saturated. If blocking a flat project with blocking wires, a circular hat or a circular lace shawl, proceed to appropriate instructions in the following section. Otherwise, lay fabric flat on a blocking board or other appropriate surface, gently coaxing project to schematic dimensions to air dry.

TECHNIQUES

Blocking Wire Method — used for flat projects with long, straight edges:
Thread blocking wires along each edge of knitted piece at regular intervals. Along side edges, you will thread blocking wires using the running threads between your selvedge stitch and its inside neighboring stitch. Thread the blocking wires through the running thread every other row for a clean, even edge. Along bind-off edges, thread the blocking wires through the right leg of every stitch in the penultimate row (this is the last row of knitting before the bind off). Along cast-on edges, thread the blocking wires through the right leg of every stitch in the first row of knitting (this is the row you worked directly into your cast on).

Pin blocking wires in place on a blocking board or other appropriate surface, using instructed dimensions. If using T-pins only, use as many pins as required to block piece into desired shape. Allow fabric to air dry completely before removing.

Hat Method — circular drying using a head form:
To create a head form, place an overturned steep-sided bowl or other appropriately-shaped object (the object should fit inside the hat) on top of an upright roll of paper towels. Place the damp hat over the head form and smooth the fabric around the edges of the form to flatten any bumps or points. Once the fabric is smooth, allow the hat to air dry until all moisture is completely gone.

Lace-Blocking Method — used for circular shawls
Lay the shawl flat on a large blocking surface. To pin the shawl into a circle, cut a piece of inelastic string a few inches longer than half the diameter (the radius) of the finished shawl (refer to schematic measurements) and anchor it to the center of the shawl with a T-pin. (For the Halo shawl on page 48, cut string to a 24 (30)" length.) From pinned center, mark four compass points (i.e. North, South, East, West) that measure a radius-length out from the center pin, using the string to make sure all are equally distant from the center pin, then mark 4 more points in between those, with the same radius. Pin the shawl out to those 8 points, with the pins at the peaks of the lace motifs. Keep adding more pins until the shawl is perfectly circular. Allow fabric to air dry completely before removing.

ABBREVIATIONS

BOR   Beginning of round

BRK   Brioche Knit; knit the next stitch together with its corresponding YO from the row below.

BRP   Brioche Purl; purl the next stitch together with its corresponding YO from the row below.

CN   Cable needle

CDD   Central Double Decrease; slip 2 stitches from L to R needle at the same time as if to k2tog, knit 1 from L needle, pass the slipped stitches over stitch just worked. (2 stitches decreased; centered)

DPN   Double-Pointed Needle

INV-L   Invisible Increase Left; Slip next stitch purlwise with yarn in back, insert tip of L needle into the L leg of stitch in the row below the stitch just slipped to R needle from back to front, lifting this stitch up onto L needle tip (the lifted stitch will sit on L needle in the wrong orientation). Knit the lifted stitch through the back loop (1 stitch increased; leans left)

INV-R   Invisible Increase Right; Insert tip of R needle into R leg of stitch below first stitch on L needle from back to front, lifting this stitch up onto L needle tip. Knit the lifted stitch, then slip the original stitch purlwise with yarn in back (1 stitch increased; leans right)

K2TOG   Knit 2 Together; knit two stitches on L needle together. (1 stitch decreased; leans right)

KFB   Knit into front and then into back of next stitch (1 stitch increased)

L   Left; used in technique instructions to indicate which of your two working needles is being used

M1   Make 1; with L needle tip, pick up the running thread between stitch just worked and first stitch on L needle from front to back. Knit the running thread through the back loop (1 stitch increased)

M1-BL   Make 1 Backward Loop; make 1 by creating a firm backward loop on R needle (1 stitch increased)

P2TOG   Purl 2 Together; purl two stitches on L needle together (1 stitch decreased; leans right)

ABBREVIATIONS

PFB	Purl into front and then into back of next stitch (1 stitch increased)
R	Right; used in technique instructions to indicate which of your two working needles is being used
RS	Right Side; refers to the public side of the knitted fabric, i.e. the fabric that will be visible when garment is worn. In projects with reversible fabrics, RS is assigned specifically at the beginning of the pattern
SSK	Slip, Slip, Knit (Modified): Slip 1 stitch knitwise from L to R needle, replace stitch on L needle in new orientation then knit two stitches together through the back loops. (1 stitch decreased; leans left)
SSP	Slip, Slip, Purl; slip 2 stitches knitwise, one at a time, transfer stitches back to L needle in their new orientation, then purl the stitches together through the back loops (1 stitch decreased; leans left)
WS	Wrong Side; refers to the non-public side of the knitted fabric, i.e. the fabric that will not be visible when garment is worn. In projects with reversible fabrics, WS is assigned specifically at the beginning of the pattern
WYIB	With yarn in back
WYIF	With yarn in front
YF-SL1-YO	Yarn Forward, Slip 1, Yarn Over; bring the working yarn under the needle to the front of the work, slip the next stitch purlwise, then bring the yarn over the needle (creating a YO on top of the slipped stitch) to the back, in position to knit the following stitch. This slipped stitch/yarn over pair is considered one stitch
YF-SL1-YOF	Yarn Forward, Slip 1, Yarn Over to Front; with yarn at the front of the work, slip the next stitch purlwise, then bring the yarn over the needle (creating a YO on top of the slipped stitch) and back to the front (under the needle), in position to purl the following stitch. This slipped stitch/yarn over pair is considered one stitch

ACKNOWLEDGMENTS

A very special thanks to my multi-talented team of collaborators who made this book possible. Elizabeth McMurtry for your steadfast project coordination and smart wardrobe styling. Robin Melanson, my senior technical editor, for your meticulous work on the patterns and techniques in this book. Christine Craig and Sue McCain for putting the first pattern drafts through your technical gauntlet. Jen Hurley for your consummate eagle eye in copy editing and your active assistance in getting this book from the screen to page. Rushada Wimer and Julia Bullard for wearing the knitting so well and inspiring such quiet, beautiful imagery. Luigi Boccia for your bottomless well of support and encouragement through every step of this process. The Lailer family for providing me with a peaceful and secluded place on the Washington coast for indulging my inner hermit when it came time to make these patterns a reality. To our talented sample knitters who bring the work to life and contributed beautiful handwork for our photoshoot. And to my extraordinary team at Brooklyn Tweed for helping keep the ship afloat each time this book took me on yet another detour.